like our SISTERS before us

WOMEN OF WISCONSIN LABOR

BY JAMAKAYA

BASED ON INTERVIEWS CONDUCTED
FOR THE WOMEN OF WISCONSIN LABOR
ORAL HISTORY PROJECT

The Wisconsin Labor History Society
Milwaukee, Wisconsin   1998

Like Our Sisters Before Us:
Women of Wisconsin Labor
By Jamakaya
© 1998 Wisconsin Labor History Society
ISBN: 0-9663267-0-9

Wisconsin Labor History Society
6333 W. Blue Mound Road
Milwaukee, WI   53213
414/771-0700

This project is funded in part by the Wisconsin Sesquicentennial Commission with funds from individual and corporate contributors and the State of Wisconsin.

Cover Photo Credits
Back cover: Evelyn Donner Day photo courtesy of Charles and Marilyn Donner; Lee Schmeling photo by Marny Malin; Joanne Bruch photo by Murray Weiss. Front cover: Alice Holz photo (upper, left) by Murray Weiss; Nellie Wilson photo (upper, right) by Murray Weiss; Catherine Conroy photo (lower, right) courtesy of the University of Wisconsin Board of Regents; Doris Thom photo (lower, left) by Murray Weiss.

Printed in Milwaukee, Wisconsin by Moser Printing Company, Inc.

Like Our Sisters Before Us

Contents

Introduction   *i*

Evelyn Donner Day   *1*

Alice Holz   *9*

Evelyn Gotzion   *17*

Catherine Conroy   *23*

Nellie Wilson   *35*

Doris Thom   *46*

Lee Schmeling   *55*

Helen Hensler   *62*

Joanne Bruch   *72*

Florence Simons   *81*

List of Interviewees   *89*

Bibliography   *92*

Photo Credits   *93*

INTRODUCTION

The Wisconsin Labor History Society's *Women of Wisconsin Labor Oral History Project* was initiated in 1988 by union women who were determined to ensure that the contributions of women to the labor movement are more fully documented.

Inspired by unionist Catherine Conroy and educator Kathryn Clarenbach, both of whom were leaders in the feminist movement in Wisconsin and nationally, the project has conducted extensive interviews with 27 women who have played important roles in their unions and their communities. They come from diverse backgrounds and represent many different occupations. Some began their union activism in the 1920's and '30's — others are continuing to make their mark today.

Like Our Sisters Before Us: Women of Wisconsin Labor features the inspiring life stories of ten of the women interviewed: Evelyn Donner Day, Alice Holz, Doris Thom, Evelyn Gotzion, Nellie Wilson, Catherine Conroy, Helen Hensler, Florence Simons, Lee Schmeling, and Joanne Bruch. Their compelling testimonies offer revealing observations about how workplaces have changed for women over the years. They convey the struggles working women have had with employers, and sometimes with their own union brothers, to gain full acceptance and respect. The women discuss: union organizing drives of the 1930's; the impact of World War II on working women; sexism and racism in the workplace; major strikes and the anti-union

i

tactics of management; the opening of jobs previously restricted to men; the "double day" — on the job and with the family at home; de-industrialization; and the impact of the feminist movement in changing both laws and attitudes about working women.

In addition to distinguished service in their unions, many of these women worked tirelessly in political campaigns and organizations like the Urban League, the Wisconsin (Allied) Council of Senior Citizens, and the National Organization for Women. Theirs is an impressive record of union solidarity and community service that deserves to be recognized.

The audio recordings, written summaries, and photos and memorabilia of the interviewees are available in a special collection entitled *Women of Wisconsin Labor* in the Archives Division of the State Historical Society of Wisconsin. A list of all the women interviewed for the project (along with their union affiliations) appears at the end of this book. We hope the collection will be used by scholars to further explore and analyze working women's contributions to Wisconsin's social and labor history. We thank the Historical Society for permission to quote from the materials now housed there.

We are painfully aware that there are many, many other pioneering union women who deserve to be interviewed. We encourage women and men in communities around the state to use their audio and/or video recorders to interview the older members of their unions. There is a great deal of experience and wisdom to be shared and a whole history of women's contributions to be recorded and celebrated. A bibliography at the end of this book suggests resources for learning about and recording oral histories.

Please consider the following notes on the text. The names of all locations in this book refer to places in the state of Wisconsin unless otherwise noted. All quotes in this book are drawn from the interviews conducted for the project or from written materials submitted to the project by the interviewees. In several cases, additional quotes were sought and included for the purpose of updating some of the women's life stories. This was necessary because some of them were interviewed as far back as 1988.

Many individuals and organizations assisted us in collecting the 27 oral histories that comprise the *Women of Wisconsin Labor Oral History Project*. Original funding was provided by the Wisconsin State

Introduction

AFL-CIO, the Wisconsin Labor History Society, the International Association of Machinists and Aerospace Workers-District 10, the United Steelworkers of America-District 2, and the Coalition of Labor Union Women-Milwaukee. Funding for this publication was provided by the Wisconsin Sesquicentennial Commission and the Wisconsin State AFL-CIO. Our thanks also go out to: Harry Miller at the State Historical Society; photographers Murray Weiss and Marny Malin; cover artist Ruth Vonderberg; proofreader Catherine Burgoyne; the good people at the Moser Printing Company; and the members of various unions who suggested women to interview and provided us with background information.

As originally conceived, the *Women of Wisconsin Labor Oral History Project* was intended to educate and inspire today's younger generation of working women and unionists — both male and female — about the path-breaking of their foresisters. Their sense of justice and fair play, their courage in taking risks, and their solidarity with fellow workers in the face of exploitation and intimidation by employers provide important examples for working people in today's rapidly changing economy.

Like our sisters before us, we have the ability to unite with fellow workers to improve our workplaces. We have the right and the responsibility to organize for just compensation, for safe work environments, and for health and pension benefits that provide security for ourselves and our families. It isn't always easy. But like our sisters before us, we know that we can stand together and demand change. Like our sisters before us, we have the power to shape our future.

Jamakaya
Women of Wisconsin Labor Oral History Project Historian

Joanne Ricca
Women of Wisconsin Labor Oral History Project Coordinator
Wisconsin Labor History Society

EVELYN DONNER DAY

*"I guess that was my nature from the very
beginning — always to take care
of the person who has less."*

✦ ✦ ✦

"I used to think it was just terrible," Evelyn Donner Day recalled about the struggle to form unions in the 1930's.

"You couldn't hardly pick up a paper without reading about some hosiery worker or union person going south and being shot dead. Soon as he'd hit the south, they'd kill him. Oh, that just irked me no end. I thought, 'something's got to be done about this,' and that's when I started to get the urge to really get in there and do something about unions."

"I gotta fight back," Evelyn explained. "When I was a little kid, I could never stand to have a bully bully a young kid or an underdog. I never allowed anyone to touch a person that was lesser than they. If they weren't as strong, I was pitching right in and fighting for 'em. I guess that was my nature from the very beginning — always to take care of the person who has less."

Milwaukeean Evelyn Donner Day distinguished herself through a long life dedicated to union activism and to advocacy on behalf of women and senior citizens. Among her many achievements, she was elected to the Executive Board of Branch 16 of the Hosiery Workers of America in the 1930's. During World War II and the 1950's, she was active in the International Ladies' Garment Workers Union (ILGWU). After finding employment at American Motors at age 50, Evelyn immersed herself in United Auto Workers (UAW) Local 75, becoming the first woman to sit on its Executive Board in the 1960's and later serving as president of its retirees' chapter. In the 1960's, she was appointed by Governor John Reynolds to the Wisconsin Commission on the Status of Women and, after her retirement, she served as assistant secretary and then president of the Allied Council of Senior Citizens.

In all of these capacities, Evelyn fought tirelessly for "the rights of the people" and was never afraid to challenge "the bosses" and other authority figures. She won notoriety in 1979 when, on a visit to the White House with a delegation of senior citizen leaders, she confronted Secretary of Health, Education and Welfare Joseph Califano about the Carter administration's failure to promote a national health insurance plan. Evelyn said that members of the State Legislature and the Milwaukee County Board of Supervisors sometimes joked in mock terror, "Here comes Evelyn!" when they saw her approaching on a lobbying mission. "They knew that I would have lashed them good," the 81-year-old activist gleefully recalled.

Young Evelyn Buckett

Evelyn Buckett was born in Milwaukee on July 3, 1908, the fifth of six children born to James and Mary Winters Buckett. Her parents were seasonal workers at the National

Evelyn Donner Day

Avenue Hatworks, but despite the sometimes tight finances, Evelyn remembered the "wonderful times" she shared with her siblings and parents. The Pilgrim's Rest Cemetery, across the street from the Bucketts' home, provided plenty of activity for the children's bodies and imaginations. Ghost stories were a big part of childhood fun, as were softball games in the city league for which James was an umpire. The Bucketts also had a large garden plot

> *"They knew that I would have lashed them good!"*

from which Mary would harvest vegetables. She would load a wagon with a variety of produce and, after school, Evelyn and her siblings embarked on a regular route through their neighborhood selling the fresh vegetables.

Evelyn's formal education consisted of kindergarten through 8th grade, after which she attended Girl's Tech for two years. Girl's Tech, the counterpart of Boy's Tech in those pre-women's liberation days, taught cooking, millinery and dressmaking skills.

"I was pretty good at school," Evelyn recalled. "I liked my school. Everybody didn't always like me because I was a little go-getter. I was always out in front doing something — very assertive about things. But they knew when I said something I said it because I meant it. That's why the company always said they could believe anything I said because I never lied to them about a thing. And I think that means a lot when you are negotiating for your own people. Lying gets you absolutely nowhere. You've got to see both sides of a picture. You've got to act on it as it should be acted on...."

Evelyn's first job was as an assistant to a milliner where she was paid 25 cents an hour. She also worked as a nurse's aide before getting a job at Phoenix Hosiery and, later, at Holeproof Hosiery. Her most vivid memories of the 1920's were not labor-related, however. She recalled with obvious delight the many dances she attended with her brothers and the many dance contests they won: "I was just a natural. And I felt so free and wonderful!" In 1928, Evelyn married Lawrence Donner, "one of the top sign writers in the city of Milwaukee," who worked for the Luick Ice Cream Company (later purchased by Sealtest). She soon left her job at Holeproof to have her children, Charles and Ronald.

Evelyn's domestic duties did not keep her home all the time though. From March to July of 1933 she walked a picket line to help win a union for employees at Luick: "Oh, I almost got arrested a couple of times. I would jump on the cars of the dealers when they would come and I would talk to them all the way in to get their ice cream, and by the time they'd get there they'd back out and they wouldn't get the ice cream.... And when we got out, there'd be a cop there waiting to take me off the car. But that didn't deter me. Believe me, I would have gone to jail."

> *"I almost got arrested a couple of times. But that didn't deter me. I would have gone to jail."*

In 1935, Evelyn went back to work at Holeproof Hosiery, which had been unionized. She signed up immediately and in a short time became a steward, handling grievances for her department. Later, she was elected an officer in Branch 16 of the Hosiery Workers of America. When she learned that the company often laid off married women, she worked hard to ensure that seniority rights regardless of marital status were included in the contract. The company should not have assumed, she said, that every married woman had another bread-winner in the home and was therefore expendable. Evelyn herself had gone back to work because her husband was an alcoholic, and she could not always depend on his income to support the family. She was a prime example of married women's needs for equal access and equal rights in the workforce.

Among her proudest achievements was the establishment of a medical plan for Holeproof workers and their families during the Depression. "I knew what it meant not to have money to be able to feed your family and take care. When I was at Holeproof they started the Milwaukee Medical Center. I was instrumental in getting that going. I got over 500 members at Holeproof to join that. Boy, that was a wonderful thing. You'd pay $1 a month and $2 for a couple, $3 for a family. You got your hospital, you got your medicines, your doctors — everything."

Evelyn credited her growing union savvy in part to the many labor classes she attended at Milwaukee's Public Library in the 1930's. Sponsored by the Milwaukee Labor Council and taught by educators and veteran unionists, the classes focused on labor history, union organizing, contract negotiations and more. One of her favorite teachers was the legendary firebrand Maud McCreery, a socialist, suffragist, labor activist and reporter whom she described as "a doll, a real humdinger." She paid tribute as well to Ruth Shapiro, who was instrumental in organizing the classes. "That's really where the history starts, right down there in those rooms," Evelyn commented.

When World War II began, Holeproof expanded with a parachute division. Women workers were asked to transfer into these new positions. Many were reluctant, but not Evelyn. She found the sewing work more interesting and the pay much better. As a parachute maker, however, her union affiliation changed. She became a member of the International Ladies' Garment Workers Union. She remained with the ILGWU through most of the 1950's when she worked at Junior House. She served as an advisor to the ILGWU Executive Board during that time.

In 1958, largely in an effort to make more money and build some security for herself and her husband, whose health was declining, Evelyn applied and was hired at American Motors. She was assigned to second shift duties in the Richards Street plant where she worked until her retirement in 1971.

"My reputation preceded me when I went to American Motors," Evelyn noted with satisfaction. "When I got there some of the boys I worked with at Holeproof said, 'Now you fellas got a woman you can run and I *know* she's gonna win. Because we had her for many, many years and we know what she's like.' And I ran, and no other woman even got through the primary, and I got elected right off the bat."

> *"My reputation preceded me when I went to American Motors."*

Like Our Sisters Before Us

Evelyn became the first woman ever to sit on the Executive Board of UAW Local 75. She was elected recording secretary twice, serving from 1963-69. She sat on the bargaining committee and attended many regional and national conventions. She was also a delegate to the Milwaukee County Labor Council for many years.

"For six years I had the advantage of being their secretary," Evelyn said of her position with Local 75, "and I was proud of every minute of it." She was most satisfied "when I saw how keenly the people were interested in [union business].... Naturally, it was very satisfying when we got what we wanted for our people, but you never get everything you want. You have to be prepared to deal a little bit." She loved being in the thick of things, attending negotiations with the company and participating in many UAW conferences and events. She was particularly grateful for the opportunity to travel to meetings throughout the US and Canada.

But there were low points as well. Evelyn remembered feeling the wrath of many workers — both men and women — at the time the new federal laws on equal pay and job opportunities took effect in the

Evelyn Donner Day and colleagues on the Executive Board of UAW Local 75, 1964

Evelyn Donner Day

1960's. Many men feared their jobs would be taken by women and some women worried they would be forced to take jobs they did not want or could not perform. Evelyn felt that she became something of a scapegoat for everyone's fears at that time of change.

Evelyn also encountered blatant sexism. When she ran for office, her campaign posters were defaced. "Oh God, they were so against women," she sighed. "It was terrible." How did she surmount that barrier? It took awhile, she said, but "Once they got to respecting me for the job I was doing, I never had any problem with my men. They were all very nice."

The label "communist" was often used to discredit union activists. Evelyn said, "They tried to tag me as a communist at American Motors when I was running for office. If they can't do anything else, they'll tag you [as a communist].... I just didn't think it was fair." She ended whispers about herself by confronting head-on the individuals responsible and making it clear that she wouldn't stand for such lies.

Evelyn lost her bid for re-election as recording secretary in 1969. Shortly after that disappointment, her husband Lawrence passed away. She retired from American Motors in 1971, but became the president of its retirees' chapter and served in that position until 1985. It was at a retirees' meeting that she met Wayne Day, "an absolute jewel," who became her second husband. Evelyn's years of service to the UAW were recognized with the Walter P. Reuther Distinguished Service Award and the UAW Region 10 Solidarity Award.

She offered this perspective on the labor movement: "Today I keep praying that our unions can come back. I keep praying that people wake up and realize what they're doing by saying, 'We don't need unions today.' Because they don't know what they're saying when they say that. They really haven't gone through anything if they actually believe that.... It's as necessary now as it was in the beginning. I can't believe that the companies are getting so irresponsible as far as their workers are concerned and not giving a damn what happens to [them]. We've got to fight for every little thing we need for our people."

Evelyn remained extremely active in her retirement, primarily as the executive secretary and then president of the Allied Council of Senior Citizens of Wisconsin (now the Wisconsin Council of Senior

Citizens). She helped to build membership and local chapters throughout the state. Evelyn was proudest of the Allied Council's successful campaign to create a state ombudsman program to monitor conditions in nursing homes. The group also spearheaded the effort to establish reduced fares for the elderly on municipal transit systems.

"I had no doubts whatever that one day I would be up there really working for the people and leading," Evelyn commented just weeks before her death in March 1990. "I don't think there's anything I would have changed in my life...even all the hardship and the sorrow I went through," she concluded. "I like my life just the way it was."

Evelyn Donner Day, 1908-1990

ALICE HOLZ

*"It was an experience of cooperation
that I think is vital."*

When asked what she wanted to be when she was growing up, Alice Holz responded vociferously: *"I didn't want to be caught dead in an office!"* Then she laughed at the irony.

Alice Holz distinguished herself as an organizer of and a mainstay in Milwaukee's office workers' local from the 1930's through the 1950's and became a chief advocate and organizer of the Office and Professional Employees International Union (OPEIU). She played a pivotal role in winning the International's charter from a reluctant American Federation of Labor (AFL) in the 1940's and served as one of its first vice-presidents.

Alice, born in Milwaukee on December 8, 1912, was strongly influenced by her parents, Christian and Alma Holz. Her father, a Socialist Party member, was a conscientious objector during World War I and later ran (unsuccessfully) for a seat on the Milwaukee City Council. Christian Holz operated a barber shop at 26th Street and Lisbon Avenue where customers were treated to political discussions on socialism and labor organizing along with their haircuts. Alice recalled her mother's "deep sense of justice" and credited her with implementing many of her father's plans and campaigns.

"Whatever activities my father engaged in meant that his whole family became a part of that activity," Alice said. From a very young age, Alice and her younger brother Marvin distributed handbills, canvassed door-to-door, and attended lectures by Socialist Party leaders. Prominent socialists and labor activists from across the US and Europe came to visit Christian Holz, whose children were duly impressed. Although she and her brother sometimes had to endure the taunts of children who called them "reds," Alice described her childhood and adolescence as filled with "rich experiences which gave us education in many different ways.... We grew up in an atmosphere of experience, an atmosphere of intellect, of being a part of society and contributing to society."

After graduating in 1931 from West Division High School, Alice faced an "unhappy period" in her life. The family had no money to send her to college and, in the depths of the Depression, she was unable to find work. To keep herself busy, Alice took typing and shorthand courses at vocational school. She also volunteered at Brisbane Hall, headquarters of the Socialist Party and many labor unions in Milwaukee. She eventually worked part-time in the circulation department of *The Milwaukee Leader*, the Socialist newspaper. While working at Brisbane Hall, she became involved in the leftist politics and union organizing that flourished in the mid-1930's. Alice recalled: "I was very impressed with the intelligence and loyalty of many of the early members of the labor movement." Among those she befriended were Maud McCreery and Harold "Hap" Beck.

> *"I was very impressed with the intelligence and loyalty of many of the early members of the labor movement."*

Because she had been doing typing and office work for the Socialist Party, Alice joined Office Workers Local 16456 in 1935. The following year, she found full-time employment as secretary to Truck Drivers Local 347. Her hiring was something of a victory for the office workers' local because the truck drivers said they did not want to hire from the office workers' union — a wife or daughter of one of the drivers was likely to get the job. But the office workers' union, shocked at the lack of solidarity, threatened to picket the truck drivers' local. The truck drivers backed down and hired Alice.

Her first full-time job was quite a challenge. Alice recalled: "You couldn't admit you didn't know how to make a bank deposit, how to do things. You didn't want to lose a job that you finally got after five years. You just went ahead and did it. Probably luck was with me, because the new officers of these relatively new unions — young unions — didn't know much either. So we were all growing up and learning at one time." Among Alice's duties were collecting and recording dues and processing and updating memberships. She also gained experience designing handbills and wrote articles for the newsletter. "There was something different each day, and I found this exciting," she said.

Meanwhile, "eager to become an officer," Alice ran for and won election as financial secretary of Local 16456, a position she held until 1952. She became a strong advocate for expanding the base of the office workers' local which, in the 1930's, was limited mostly to employees of labor organizations. She thought the local should try winning commercial and business contracts. "After all," she said, "here was this big, wonderful field of employees who needed us."

Organizing office workers presented many challenges, however. Companies devised many "subterfuges" to derail the organizing efforts: issuing promotions to key employees to buy their loyalty; re-classifying some workers as "confidential" employees, making them ineligible for union membership; and intimidating and red-baiting union supporters.

But some attitudes among office workers themselves proved to be hurdles. According to Alice, many office workers felt "above" the labor movement. They saw the need for unions in manufacturing or in the trades, "but saw no need for a union for office and professional employees. They felt they could get what they wanted by themselves, that their employer would recognize their aptitude. We used to say, 'the white collar strangled the office worker.'" Another hurdle to organizing at the time was the reluctance of women workers. "Women employees did not see themselves as a continuing workforce. Everybody was going to get married," Alice said. "That was the tone of the late '30's."

Despite these challenges and through much hard work, inroads were made gradually. Companies whose office workers joined Local 16456 included Miller Brewing Co., Blatz, The Transport Co. and International Harvester. During the war years, Local 16456 succeeded in organizing office workers in many of the area's plants. Their proximity to factory workers made these workers less fearful of unions and more knowledgeable about the benefits that accrued to those who joined unions, Alice noted.

Aiding Alice in these organizing efforts was the store of knowledge she obtained through attending the School for Workers at the University of Wisconsin Extension in Madison and similar labor classes in Milwaukee. Subjects included collective bargaining, parliamentary procedure and labor history. "I enjoyed every minute of labor school," Alice commented. "It was a terrific opportunity for me. What I learned in one night of school I applied to the work we were engaged in. So it was instant application of education."

She spoke warmly of her decades-long friendship with Ruth Shapiro, a Milwaukee librarian and activist in the State, County and Municipal Employees' union, who was "intensely involved" in workers' education both locally and on the national level. Ruth often carted boxes of books to the many union gatherings she attended. "In my opinion," Alice declared, "Ruth was the first Bookmobile. She was a very charming person with a wide range of friends and a tremendous amount of vitality. If one knew Ruth, one automatically was on a committee. She was a remarkable person and made a great contribution to labor."

As an officer in Local 16456, Alice attended state AFL meetings where she spoke with delegates from other office workers' locals. Although directly affiliated with the AFL, they were all independent unions with no unified administration or international union of their own. Alice determined to change this by starting an office workers' council, the first step in forming an international union.

"The Milwaukee office workers' union made many, many petitions to the AFL asking for a council to be established," Alice recalled. "We would get into communication with several different office worker locals in the state and say, 'Write to President William Green, urging him to set the motions in progress to set up a council.' But it was a long, long time, and President Green usually responded by saying: 'This is not the time to establish an office workers' council.'"

"Throughout the US, more and more office workers' unions were being established. [It took] a great deal of insistence — not only did we write to President Green but we wrote to all the state federations of labor, getting all their friends to write to the AFL and its Executive Board to consider the proposition of establishing a council."

"A council is really a probationary period for a group of similar local unions before the establishment of an international union. When President Green called a conference in Detroit [in 1942] for the office workers' locals throughout the country and Canada to consider the establishment of a council, I was elected a delegate. I served on the by-laws committee and we worked out a constitution for the council. I was elected to the Executive Board of the International Council, and I served on the different committees and helped formulate procedures and policies."

Alice Holz (center, behind charter) and colleagues accepting the OPEIU charter, 1945 (Photo courtesy OPEIU)

Like Our Sisters Before Us

Finally, in January 1945, the AFL granted a charter to the Office Employees International Union ("Professional" was later added to the title). Alice, who played such a key role in its foundation, was elected a regional vice-president of the International Union and immersed herself in the policy-making and organizing of its early years.

At about this time, Alice left her job with the truck drivers' union and became secretary to the Regional Director of the AFL. The regional office worked directly with hundreds of federal labor unions in Wisconsin and the upper Midwest, assisting them with organizing, negotiations, elections and other internal affairs. Alice found the diversity of the unions her office dealt with "fascinating," and the job provided her with many new and exciting learning experiences. She worked briefly for Regional Director David Sigman and then with his successor, Jacob Friedrick.

"If I had a mentor, I would say that Jake was mine," Alice commented. "Jake was a very quiet individual and a very thoughtful individual. He gave whatever problem we as office workers had very careful attention and did it in a very objective way. We had an extremely good working relationship."

Alice's responsibilities to her job with the AFL and her position with the OPEIU sometimes resulted in 12, even 14-hour days. She enjoyed traveling and meeting people, learning about other unions and, along the way, learning much more about labor law, contract negotiations — the nitty-gritty of union business. The only really burdensome times she experienced were those periods when unions became embroiled in jurisdictional disputes, which she compared to "bitter family feuds," and the time in the late 1940's when this proud daughter of socialists was forced to declare her "loyalty."

"Loyalty oaths were demanded by legislation," Alice explained. "The principle officers of a labor union had to sign the loyalty oath to the effect that you were not a Communist." As an officer of the local and a vice-president of the International union, this caused Alice "a great deal of personal anxiety. I opposed, as many others in the labor movement did, having to sign such a statement. On the other hand, had I not signed, the government could keep us from processing our elections. I finally resolved this by saying 'I will sign the statement only because as an officer I can function, and our local union and the International can function.' It was a personally difficult time for me

Alice Holz

Alice Holz, 1989

as it was for many others. Because I took my integrity as very important, and I just felt that signing that statement was totally against my principles."

Alice experienced gender bias throughout her union career. In the 1930's she was denied a scholarship to a labor school because it was assumed a man would make better use of the skills acquired. As an officer of her local and the International, "Employers would be very surprised that a woman came to represent the office employees," Alice said. She won them over with her knowledge and professionalism. Though Alice was a longtime employee of several unions, "there was never any opportunity or even any talk of offering [me] a staff position. That was really territory that was just *not*, in the unions' opinion, *not* for women."

She was greatly heartened in recent years by the new opportunities available to women both in the labor movement and in the workforce as a whole. "I cannot express to you the joy that I have when I hear of all these new, wonderful careers that women can get into. I know it's not easy," Alice said philosophically, "but it's more open."

Asked if she felt her leadership role in the labor movement paved the way for other women, Alice commented: "How can I say that I paved the way? I can't say that personally. I think that women's involvement came about because women insisted on it. It takes the concerted effort of all, not just one. There were more before me...."

Alice did not seek re-election as International vice-president after her second term, and in 1952 she relinquished her position as financial secretary of Local 16456 (which, since its affiliation with OPEIU, had become Local 9): "There comes a time when one becomes very tired. I had spent so much time with the office workers to the exclusion of almost everything else. I definitely felt it was time to let go." This withdrawal coincided with her leaving the AFL regional office as well. After eight years of employment there she still had no pension or health insurance. Entering middle age, she felt the need for greater security. She worked several years for Brewery Workers Local 9 and then accepted an even better offer from Teamsters Local 344, where she served as office manager until her retirement in 1978. She expressed pride at having set up the health, welfare and pension departments for Local 344.

Asked if she had any regrets about her union work, Alice replied: "I suppose I regret some errors in judgment. I'm certainly sorry we don't have hundreds of thousands of people in the office workers' union, but I'm philosophical about that. I realize, through my father's teaching, that history isn't made in a day."

Interviewed just months before her death in 1990, Alice said: "I am sure that I had more excitement during my working years as an employee in the labor union than probably any other occupation I might have gone into. Each day I never knew what I was finally going to do or accomplish that day. It was a challenge. I was never bored, probably for the 43 years I worked in the labor movement."

It was also, she said, "an experience of cooperation that I think is vital.... It was an experience in helping one another and learning from one another and really caring for one another that would not have occurred had I been in private industry. I treasure the friendships I made throughout all those years in the labor movement. So all in all, I think I have been extemely lucky."

EVELYN GOTZION

*"Oh, we had a lot of heartaches,
a lot of fun."*

"I think the union was the greatest thing that ever happened in my day," Evelyn Gotzion declared. "I certainly was happy to have it because I knew that if you had a grievance, you had something wrong, you had a place to go with it. You could thrash it out, you had somebody to help you straighten it out. Nowadays if you don't have a union, where do you go, what do you do?"

Evelyn Gotzion worked for more than 40 years at the Rayovac battery plant in Madison. In the 1930's, she played a central role organizing Rayovac workers into Federal Labor Union 19587. She served on its bargaining committee for 30 years, slowly gaining pay raises and health and pension benefits from the notoriously anti-union company. Evelyn was a longtime advocate of affiliation with the United Auto Workers, which finally came about in 1963, when FLU 19587 was transformed into UAW Local 1329. Evelyn was also a delegate to the Madison Federation of Labor for 25 years, during which time she participated in the many activities and debates of the local labor movement. She recalled her union days as a time of both laughter and tears.

Like Our Sisters Before Us

Evelyn Bailey was born in Dane County on May 8, 1913, one of fourteen children born to Alfred and Ella Paul Bailey. She spent her childhood years on the family farm owned by Grandfather Bailey, helping her mother and supervising her siblings. She speculated that she may have developed her mediation skills and her concern for fellow workers because of her family responsibilities: "I think when you have a big family you're always helping them. You're always waiting on them and trying to do things for them. You become motherly before you are a mother."

Evelyn completed 8th grade and then attended vocational school for awhile. At age 16, she got a job working in the dining room of a hospital. She worked there until she married her husband, Steve Gotzion, in 1930. They had three children: Doris, Dean and David.

Evelyn started work at Rayovac in the 1930's. In the depths of the Depression, "You were so happy to have a job no matter what it was," she commented. The plant was located close to her and Steve's home, which enabled Evelyn to come home over noon hours to check on the children who were left in the care of her sister.

"But it was very dirty," she said of the Rayovac plant. "It was a very bad place to work. It was so dirty because of all this carbon in the batteries. When you came home at night you had to immediately take a bath, and if you didn't cover your hair, you'd have to wash your hair and your clothes. But we were so happy to have that job and 27 cents an hour — that's what I started with."

Evelyn began working at Rayovac just as a union organizing drive was gaining momentum. Rayovac had initiated its own "employee association" back in the 1920's, but Evelyn said most workers realized it was there to look after the interests of the company rather than those of the workers. In May 1934, the American Federation of Labor granted Federal Charter 19587 to Rayovac workers, but it took almost three more years of struggle before the company signed its first union shop contract. In those years, union organizers were laid off or fired (later to be reinstated), and strike threats were used to put pressure on Rayovac. Evelyn played a major role during this time signing up her fellow workers for the union.

"When the union started to come in there, they asked me to be a steward right away and I said 'yes' because I figured there were so many things that needed to be corrected I was willing to do it,"

Evelyn Gotzion

Evelyn recalled. "Before we had a union there were a lot of problems. They'd have work who they wanted to work whether they deserved it or not."

Indeed, the company laid off and transferred workers arbitrarily with no consideration for seniority or any other consistent criteria. Wages were low, and no health insurance, pension plan or other benefits were offered at the time. Plant conditions were dirty and dangerous.

"You had to take time to try to explain to people how much better their life could be if they had a little bit of rights where they worked," Evelyn noted. "And after that, when we got the grievance procedure, that was the greatest thing that ever came in there. Because there [were] a lot of nice, hard-working people that were very quiet and they wouldn't do anything that was wrong. *But they were so walked over!* And I didn't like that. I thought, 'We all earn our place in life and we should have it.'"

> *"You had to take time to explain how much better their life could be if they had a little bit of rights where they worked."*

Once the union shop was secured, Rayovac continued its hardball tactics, however. Evelyn said that pay raises came only "by the pennies" from contract to contract, and health insurance was "slow in coming too. They just didn't want to open the door. It was rough. It was a hard time getting there." A pension plan was only won after a bitter 19-week strike in 1963. Even then, many workers found the pension inadequate.

World War II had a dramatic effect on the Rayovac plant and on Evelyn's union involvement. She remembered: "We were *very* busy. Sometimes we would have a day off after seven days. Ten hours a day we worked a lot of the times. We worked on Thanksgiving and Christmas. And we had buttons with our pictures on it [to show] at the gate. Even if they knew you, you were supposed to wear that button at all times. And we had so many more government people in there inspecting things — and rate setters."

Like Our Sisters Before Us

One grievance during the war years thrust Evelyn into a position on her union's bargaining committee, where she stayed for the next 25 years.

"They cut our rates, and I couldn't see any reason for cutting it," Evelyn explained. "I had asked for three different rate setters to come and tell us why they had done it, and they didn't. So I said, 'Well, next thing I'm gonna do is shut the line off 'til I get some attention.' So I shut the line off and everybody said, 'My God, how'd you ever have the nerve enough to do that?' 'Well,' I said, 'I made up my mind that right's right, we're fighting for it and *we're gonna get it!*'"

"So we wrote up a grievance and every one of us signed it," she continued. Her union president asked her to join the bargaining committee to argue the case herself. "I said, 'I sure will!' So I went over there and here stands this great big guy towering over me from the company. I said, 'Let's be fair. You can't do that to people. Why are you cutting them? I mean, that hurts. They've all worked so hard and they've learned their jobs so good. They put out a lot of

Evelyn Gotzion, 1992

-20-

production and that's what you're wanting. And because you think they're making a little more money than they ought to be, that's no way to punish them.' Well anyhow, it went on and on, and we had night meetings and we had afternoon meetings and we brought in guys from Milwaukee and all over. Finally, we won it. And the people got their back pay from every hour that they were cut back. Then I stayed on the bargaining committee and I was never voted out after that. I stayed until I retired. Oh, we had a lot of heartaches, a lot of fun."

Sometimes fellow workers could be critical. "I always used to say when someone made a lot of remarks: 'Put that guy's name in for next year. We'll vote him in and see what he can do.' That's how one guy got to be president — Elmer Davis. He gave us a real bad time and I said, 'Elmer, if you think you can push things better than we do and if you've got the know-how to do it, we want you on the committee.... But he got to be a very good president. He said he learned the hard way," she chuckled.

One of the colleagues she most admired was Bill Skaar, an organizer of FLU 19587 and its president in the late 1940's and '50's. "He knew all the laws and was great to have at the bargaining table. He knew just what he was talking about," said Evelyn, though she noted he "had a short wick at times — he didn't always have the kindest way to say things." Asked if she had played the diplomat, Evelyn joked: "Well, I tried to keep peace in our family, but sometimes our family didn't always agree."

Evelyn considered running for president but decided against it. "I felt like I had my children and that it was a really important job to be a president. You should be able to answer to [members] when they wanted you any time." Evelyn said that "just being on the bargaining committee" was a lot of responsibility. "When I was bargaining, it was a lot of hours, a lot of days, a lot of evenings — that's why a lot of people don't want to get involved." She worried too that "I never had enough education." Yet, she credited the School for Workers at the University of Wisconsin Extension with teaching her many "interesting and helpful" skills for dealing with the company.

Was her husband supportive of her union activity? "My husband was *real good*. If he hadn't been so good and so good with the children, I couldn't have done all the things that I've done. I couldn't go to conventions and come home and have everything be okay."

Like Our Sisters Before Us

FLU 19587 was affiliated with the AFL from its beginnings in the 1930's, but workers in many other Rayovac plants were part of the United Auto Workers. Unionists at the Madison plant tried to change their affiliation several times and finally succeeded in 1963 when FLU 19587 relinquished its charter and transformed into UAW Local 1329. Evelyn pushed for the change, and she enumerated the advantages.

"The UAW could do more service for us because they had so many of our plants and we had a lot more pressure to put on the company. It made us a lot stronger," Evelyn said. The UAW provided more technical assistance with grievances and bargaining. It offered classes for training stewards. Better communication with UAW locals in other Rayovac plants was helpful in dealing with management. Coordinating the expiration dates of contracts — which took some time — gave Local 1329 more leverage. "That all helped," she said.

Evelyn was a delegate to the Madison Federation of Labor, the coordinating body for local unions, for many years. She relished the opportunity to learn about other unions and to exchange information with activists. She was a witness to and participant in the long debate over the location and size of the new Labor Temple. She served on the Federation's political education committee, helping to decide which candidates to support and working to get out the labor vote. She was a tireless campaign worker herself, often canvassing door-to-door in her own ward for her favorite candidates, including longtime State Senator Fred Risser. She was a mainstay at all the Federation's events, volunteering her time generously.

Evelyn's biggest disappointment over the years was "probably not getting what we wanted in our contract." Rayovac was "a tough company. They're not easy to deal with. They're hard. We didn't get all the things we wanted always but we made a little progress each year and that helped.... I've heard from people who work in the plant today that things are much better. Maybe what we did all those years ago helped a little."

Her greatest satisfaction? "I know that having the union was the most important, but I think all the wonderful people that went with it were great, too. Because we were all heading toward the same goal and fighting together. Though we all came from different walks of life, when it came right down to it, everybody was united."

CATHERINE CONROY

*"You either do what you believe in
and think is important,
or you just cave in.
And I'm not the type to do that."*

"I've always described my job as a firefighter," Catherine Conroy said of her many years as a union president and a staff representative for the Communications Workers of America (CWA). "If there was a fire, and we had 'em every day — somebody's been fired, a new policy comes out of management and it turns out to be a terrible problem — you know, we were always fighting fires."

Catherine Conroy was a leading figure in Wisconsin's labor and women's movements for four decades. She held many elective and appointive positions in her union, in women's organizations and on government advisory boards. She was a founder of the National Organization for Women (NOW), the Coalition of Labor Union Women (CLUW) and the Wisconsin Women's Network. She was a mentor to dozens of union members and feminist activists. She joked that because of her pioneering roles she was "labor's token woman and the women's movement's token labor person." Her primary legacy is the alliance she forged between organized labor and women.

Like Our Sisters Before Us

Catherine was born on November 27, 1919 in a ward for unwed mothers at Misericordia Hospital in Milwaukee. As an infant, she was adopted by James and Amelia Conroy, a couple who had been unable to have their own child. The Conroys raised her as their own in a series of homes on Milwaukee's west side. Amelia, called May, told her daughter the full story of her adoption only when Catherine was middle-aged. "I'd kind of suspected it for some time," Catherine said. "But it was alright. They were wonderful parents and I always thought of them as my own. The news didn't really cause me any great distress."

James Conroy, of English and Irish descent, was born in Milwaukee's old Third Ward. May was born in Fargo, North Dakota. She was the daughter of homesteaders who later moved back to Milwaukee. James and May married at ages 18 and 19, respectively. James became an art dealer, specializing in paintings and antiques. May worked in a millinery shop and, later, took child care jobs. "My parents were very gentle people," Catherine recalled. "My mother was the gentlest woman in the world. Discipline in my family consisted of looking at me. My mother just had to look at me and shake her head and I was guilt-ridden to death about whatever I did that I shouldn't have done."

"The famous Great Depression made a lot of problems for my family," Catherine said. "My father's business was not going well and the crash really killed it. My father was a very proud Irishman who would not go on welfare. He ended up owing everybody in the world a total of $5,000, which at that time was a fortune. Trying to find work and struggling to somehow manage took up all our energy."

Catherine was busy with school during those years, graduating from West Division High School in 1938. "I was not good college material," Catherine confessed. "I didn't have a lot of patience with classes." She found many subjects boring and so "just endured it." She did love sports, however, and she played baseball and basketball as often as she could. "I majored in extracurricular activities," she joked.

Even if Catherine had been intent on college, lack of funds would have prevented her attendance. Instead, after high school, Catherine set about looking for work. "You couldn't get a job anywhere at that time unless you knew somebody," Catherine noted. So, with the help of a friend of her father, she was hired as kitchen help at a county financed tuberculosis sanitarium. She was soon transferred to County General Hospital where she worked in the cafeteria and then in the diet kitchen, preparing special food trays for patients. She worked there for almost four years.

At these jobs, young Catherine observed the "pecking order in the health field, with doctors at the top sort of god-like, and the levels below that, each profession in their proper order down to the kitchen people and maids and all the rest who apparently weren't very important." She became especially aware of and angered by the treatment of the student nurses who she said were "terrorized" by the doctors and subject to demeaning comments. Catherine wondered what right they had to treat people that way. For her own part, "I didn't expect to be abused, and I guess it's safe to say that I was very verbal. I could defend myself." At one

> *"My consciousness of unions really didn't go anywhere until I worked at the telephone company."*

point she inquired about a union for kitchen workers — the chefs had their own union — but didn't press it: "My consciousness of unions really didn't go anywhere until I worked at the telephone company."

With the onset of World War II, more jobs became available, and Catherine's parents encouraged her to apply at the phone company where several relatives had found steady employment. She was hired by Wisconsin Bell in 1942 and worked as an operator at the long distance office. "This was prior to computers," Catherine said. "This was prior to total dial also. We still had a number of offices where the operator all day long said, "Number please. Thank you," and plugged into a current connecting one customer to another." Catherine found the work so dull that after one year she transferred into the training department, where she trained other operators.

"If I hadn't had the opportunity to get away from that board, I think I would have quit because I couldn't stand it," Catherine declared. "My knees couldn't stand it. The system had it down to such a time and motion study routine. Where you put your hands and how you put your feet on the floor and how you sat — everything was programmed. I didn't respond well to that. I was criticized because I slouched in my chair, crossed my legs. To keep from going to sleep, I played little games with myself. I found that if I put the tip of the cord against a piece of the board and pushed the ringing key I could make sparks, and that was kind of fun. It didn't hurt anything but of course it wasn't in the program."

Catherine recoiled from the regimentation and the rules. "The paternalism was just so bad," Catherine said. "It was kind of the Mother Bell family. Everyone was expected to conform. They told us how to look. They told us how to act. They even told us how to vote. There was no tolerance for any misbehaving or breaking of the rules. Absence was the worst sin you could commit short of burning the building down. They didn't fire you so fast, but they nagged you to death, and that interference in every move you made and everything you did really turned me off."

> *"The paternalism was just so bad. Everyone was expected to conform."*

Catherine inquired about a union and learned there was indeed an operators' union, but it was almost inactive. The few meetings it held featured gossip rather than workplace issues. Many of the telephone workers' unions at the time had been set up by the company itself as "employee associations." As such, they existed more as a means of controlling workers than advocating their interests. However, there was a more active union representing the craftsmen (linemen, installers, repairmen). It began raiding the operators' union seeking members to help establish a more independent union. After consulting with both groups, Catherine joined with the insurgents, who managed to gather enough signatures to win an election overseen by the National Labor Relations Board. Catherine worked with others to develop by-laws and a structure for the new union which became part of the Wisconsin Telephone Guild. She served as steward for the local at the long distance toll office.

Catherine Conroy

In 1947, the Bell System refused to negotiate with the National Federation of Telephone Workers (NFTW), which represented many of the independent telephone workers' unions, including the Wisconsin Guild. Telephone workers around the country went out on a strike that lasted for six weeks. Catherine lived just two blocks from the toll office where she worked so she became a picket captain, in charge of scheduling picketers and keeping them orderly. She said the strike magnified the need for a better organized union. The NFTW was a loose federation of independent state units and locals but had no enforcement powers. Many smaller units collapsed under the pressure of the strike. "We were fighting for the existence of the union. When it was all over," Catherine said of the strike, "it was clear at the next convention that we had to re-structure the union, for sure."

Catherine became immersed in the organizing of the new national telephone workers' union which was chartered in 1949 as the Communications Workers of America. "It was a very dramatic thing," she said of the CWA's creation. "Everybody had their own little turf, you know. We had presidents in all these little unions and they had to give that up and become part of a division of the new union.... We developed a single union with a new name and a constitution that put the power and the responsibility for negotiating contracts into the hands of an Executive Board rather than separate unions. In that process I had gone from local steward to the first convention of this new set-up to a business agent, responsible for the operating forces and the clerical forces in the Milwaukee area. I had a small geographical area, but a lot of members to worry about."

"I was young enough not to know what doesn't work," Catherine said, "so I tried everything. We rewrote the by-laws at least ten times.... Trying to put a union together was a marvelous experience for me because I really was learning with the gang what unions are about and finding out whether I could get people to work together and do all these things. I found it very exciting."

Catherine had worked as an operator and trainer for five years, after which she was given three years' leave to work for the union. When her leave time was exhausted in 1950, she had to make a decision. "I decided I didn't think that I could work for Bell full-time for the rest of my life, so I decided to take my chances with the union," Catherine said. "By that time my local knew me so well that anything I wanted was fine with them." She won election as president of Local 5500 (later, 4600) in 1951 and was re-elected until 1960, when she accepted a staff position with the national CWA.

"I was really genuinely concerned," Catherine said of the workers she represented. "I felt the operator was the most abused employee in the system, and it really aggravated me. So I was filing grievances all the time on behalf of our members, and I tried to get after the way the system operated. I didn't understand why the operator seemed to have the worst job. I didn't get the whole picture during the time I was president of that local because it was the only kind of worker I was dealing with. When I became a member of the staff and I had the responsibility for top level grievances for all the members in the eastern half of Wisconsin and I began to deal with our fellows about their problems, I thought, I'm spending all my time on

Catherine Conroy and colleagues at the CWA convention in Wausau, 1950

the problems of these guys and they're so — most of them, compared to operators' problems — so trivial. But by God, those guys made sure they got what they wanted, while the operator sits and suffers.... It was very disturbing to me and it began to occur to me that this must be a problem women have. We just can't seem to realize that the Lord helps those who help themselves, and if you don't do anything, you are going to suffer."

"I used to go to meetings and accuse them of it: 'You get this outrageous treatment. You are so regimented and confined and expected to really produce to a degree that's almost inhuman. And your solution to that problem is to go into a restroom and cry. And then, having had a good cry, you feel better. It didn't change anything, but you're ready to endure it some more. You have a union — *use it!* It's the vehicle that will solve some of these problems.' Well, we did get some solved, but it continued to frustrate me."

Catherine came to believe that the mistreatment of operators was part of a larger, institution-wide practice of gender discrimination: "The whole history of the Bell System has demonstrated — including the EEOC [Equal Employment Opportunity Commission] study of how the Bell System tracked people when they hired them — that men went in one door to one office and women went in the other. And women got just so far in the system on any kind of job. All the best jobs, all the top jobs, all second level, third level, fourth level, fifth level [jobs], were always male — always. And the only jobs women could get beyond the job they were hired for was usually a minor supervisory job, and then they were told they had a great job, but they really had no power. Women never, *never* participated in making policy. And even today, very few women, maybe half of 1% in the system, have management jobs that make policy. There are women craftpeople — women who install telephones — so there are women who have some of the better worker jobs, but that's still a token group."

Asked how black women fared at the telephone company, Catherine said she knew of only one black woman working there in the 1940's, and "the only thing they let her operate was the elevator." Things have changed, she added wryly, "Now black women are enjoying the same discrimination white women enjoy. They are still having trouble getting up there."

One personnel manager admitted to Catherine that women were treated poorly because they let the company treat them that way. "That's the way it is, and you're not going to change it," he said. Catherine replied, "I'm gonna keep trying."

Catherine's growing consciousness about discrimination against women in the workforce coincided with the resurgence of feminist activism in the 1960's. Her experience representing mostly women workers at the telephone company fueled her involvement in many feminist groups for the next 25 years.

The first influential women's group Catherine became involved with was the newly created Wisconsin Governor's Commission on the Status of Women in 1963. Kathryn "Kay" Clarenbach, a political science professor at the University of Wisconsin, was the chair of this commission. "Kay conscientiously looked for women from all around the state, from all walks of life, minority women. She was really conscientious about having a truly representative commission." Catherine was appointed as a representative of labor.

"If there was such a thing as a mentor for me," Catherine said, "although I was older than Kay, she was it. Because she knew all about the women's movement from way, way back before her day. Kay was a real inspiration, the mother of the whole movement, who took Betty Friedan's ideas and made them happen." (Friedan, author of **The Feminine Mystique**, is often credited with inspiring the second wave of feminism.)

"I think the Wisconsin commission was probably one of the best in the country," Catherine asserted. While some commissions steered away from controversy to examine topics like traffic safety, the Wisconsin commission tackled critical women's issues like pay equity, domestic violence, divorce and marital property reform. Research conducted by the commission led to the enactment of many legislative and regulatory reforms in the 1960's, '70's and '80's.

In June 1966, at a meeting of all the state commissions in Washington, DC, participants were prevented from adopting resolutions by an official of the Labor Department, the sponsoring organization. It was a clear attempt to de-politicize the commissions, and it angered some participants, including Catherine. Returning to the hotel after a late dinner, Catherine ran into Kay Clarenbach, who told her: "We've been invited to a meeting in Betty Friedan's room."

Catherine Conroy

*Catherine Conroy (left) is joined by friends (clockwise from top) Kathryn Clarenbach, Mary Jean Collins and Gene Boyer as Catherine is honored as Milwaukee NOW's Woman of the Year. (Photo © **The Milwaukee Journal Sentinel Inc.**, July 9, 1978)*

Catherine recalled the room was smoke-filled and crowded with women. "There was big conversation about the fact that we have no organization that works entirely for women's issues, and that we can't look to governors' commissions because they are under the control of a political body of some kind." Nothing was resolved that night, but the next morning the dissidents spread the word about the new organization which Betty Friedan named the National Organization for Women. Catherine, with her experience in organization-building, challenged the women to "put their money where their mouth is" by donating $5 each to establish a treasury. Friedan was named president and Kay Clarenbach was named chair, with the task of setting up a headquarters in her office in Madison. This is how NOW was born. Catherine described the first organizing meeting and the early conventions of NOW as "chaotic" and "disastrous." The problem was lack of structure, and Catherine and other union women were able to make many practical suggestions for organizing the group. In 1968, while stationed in Chicago on assignment for the CWA, Catherine established NOW's Chicago chapter and served as its first president. She organized some of its first actions, including sit-ins at "men only" grilles and "Women's Strike Day" in 1970. "Those were very exciting times," she said.

In 1974, she was again in the vanguard, attending the founding convention of the Coalition of Labor Union Women in Chicago. Catherine set up CLUW's Milwaukee chapter and served as its first president. The group's purpose was to share skills and build solidarity among women in many different unions. Later in the 1970's, Catherine was appointed by President Jimmy Carter to his Advisory Committee on Women.

In the 1970's, as her commitment to the women's movement deepened, Catherine became increasingly frustrated at the lack of women in leadership positions in her union, the CWA. In a union that was 50% women, only about 25 of the 150 staff people were female, and no women sat on its Executive Board.

"One of the arguments about women not being on the board, which was a serious concern to me, was that we don't run," Catherine said. "How can you get elected if you don't run? I thought, well I'll cure that one. So I ran. I was the first woman to run for the national Executive Board competitively." She ran for vice-president twice. Her buttons read: "CC for VP." During her campaigns, some men and women told her bluntly that they didn't believe a woman could handle the job or negotiate effectively with management. Catherine lost both elections, but was satisfied in knowing that she helped to open the way for women after her who succeeded in being elected.

Catherine had better luck when she ran for the Executive Board of the Wisconsin State AFL-CIO in 1974. She won that election, becoming the first woman to sit on the board.

Catherine Conroy

At about this time, Catherine was stunned when she was overlooked for the position of CWA state director in favor of a man who, she believed, had considerably less experience. Convinced that it was "clearly sex discrimination," Catherine appealed to the president of the CWA, who defended the man's appointment. Hoping for some change of heart, she waited 179 days, one day short of the legal limit for filing a complaint, and finally submitted a sex discrimination complaint to the Department of Industry, Labor and Human Relations and the EEOC. She said she "hated" having to file the charge. Colleagues accused her of disloyalty.

"I explained to people, 'Look, I am a feminist. I believe we have to fight for equality. Women are discriminated against. This, to me, is clearly a case of discrimination. So I'm either compelled to file a charge and fight, or shut up about women's rights.'" Catherine, interviewed in 1988, was clearly still pained by the memory of this conflict. But she wanted people to understand her position: "If we

*Catherine Conroy at home, 1974 (Photo © **The Milwaukee Journal Sentinel**, Inc., October 16, 1974)*

don't tolerate discrimination by companies, we certainly shouldn't tolerate discrimination by the organizations that are supposed to protect our rights. I know I made some people mad, but I think my challenge taught the [CWA] an important lesson — and made it a better union."

Catherine's complaint was only resolved in 1982 when she accepted a monetary settlement from the CWA at the time of her retirement.

Before her retirement, she helped win a big settlement from the telephone company on behalf of women who had been denied maternity benefits. She sent announcements of a potential class action suit along with all the requisite forms to union locals seeking the participation of women who were denied benefits. Within a year, more than 100 complaints had been submitted. A lawsuit was filed, which took years to resolve, and Wisconsin Bell ended up paying four to six weeks' wages and benefits to each of the plaintiffs, who, Catherine reported, were "thrilled" to get their checks.

Catherine retired in 1982, intent on being "able to do what I really wanted to do." Her retirement years were a flurry of activity. She became a major activist in the Wisconsin Women's Network, a coalition of women's groups that filled the void left by the disbanding of the Commission on the Status of Women. She was appointed to the Department of Natural Resources Board and the University of Wisconsin Board of Regents, where she fought successfully for the establishment of a graduate program in Nursing. She worked tirelessly on Democratic political campaigns and hosted gatherings of young union women in her home during which she listened to their concerns and offered friendly counsel.

Catherine succumbed to cancer on February 19, 1989 at age 69. Betty Friedan, speaking to the *The Milwaukee Journal*, called Catherine "one of our heroines," and paid tribute to "her spirit, her courage, her humor, her shrewdness and realism." Ann Crump, a telephone worker Catherine took "under her wing" who is now herself a staff representative for the CWA, said of her mentor: "Catherine's advice to so many young pups like myself was invaluable. It's now up to us to carry on her work — to seek justice in the workplace and in society as a whole."

NELLIE WILSON

*"When you know that you're the bridge that takes
somebody over,
that's a really good feeling."*

Nellie Wilson, a self-described "thorn in the side of
management," was hired in 1943 by Milwaukee's A.O. Smith
Corporation and worked there as a precision inspector, assembly line
worker, machine operator and shipping and receiving clerk until 1969.
She was an outspoken steward (1960-62) and the first African
American woman elected to the Executive Board of the Smith
Steelworkers Local 19806 (1964-69).

Nellie was a delegate to the Milwaukee County Labor Council
(1961-69), a member of the State AFL-CIO committees on women
and civil rights, and established a civil rights committee in her own
local. Hired as area representative for the AFL-CIO's Human
Resources Development Institute in 1971, Nellie helped place the
unemployed in apprenticeships and union shops. She retired in 1983
after Reagan-era budget cuts undermined the program.

Nellie Sweet was born on November 28, 1916 in Lufkin, Texas.
Her mother died of tuberculosis when Nellie was just three, and while
her father worked to "find himself," Nellie spent her childhood years

on her grandparents' farm, 100 acres owned "free and clear" near the small town of Alto. She spoke nostalgically of the cycles of planting and harvesting on the farm, and of the endless canning of peaches, apples, figs, peas, tomatoes, and blackberries. Her grandmother carded and spun cotton and sewed all the family's clothes. In the absence of a doctor, she collected herbs and mixed the teas and compounds needed for medicinal use.

"Education was very important to those people in those days," Nellie said. She attended school every day and read many of her uncle's books by the light of an oil lamp in the evenings. "I had a better education when I finally left that farmhouse than most kids my age did because I was into the classics."

She also learned about the racist order of Texas at a young age. Family members rarely ventured into town, only for supplies and only when it was "absolutely necessary." Nellie's grandfather was an ex-slave and, although he didn't talk about it much, she recalled references to "masters." Once, she was severely chastised by her grandfather for singing "Marching Through Georgia" (the Union's anthem, "Battle Hymn of the Republic"). Black people had been lynched for much lesser supposed transgressions. "You don't sing 'Marching Through Georgia' in Texas in 1920, period!" she recalled.

In 1928, after her grandparents died, Nellie's father moved with her to Milwaukee where he found work as an iron molder at International Harvester. "He was so proud of himself because he had a trade," Nellie commented. Durham Sweet was a union member and also active in Marcus Garvey's Negro Improvement Association and the National Association for the Advancement of Colored People.

"He taught me to be independent," Nellie said of her father. "He taught me not to sit and envy something that somebody else had — if I wanted it, to get up and get it for myself. [Because of him] I've always liked to read. I'm inquisitive. I'm interested in what goes on around me too. I've learned through bitter experience how politics affects our lives."

The move to Milwaukee was a difficult transition for young Nellie, whose thick southern accent made her self-conscious among her new classmates at Highland Avenue School. She soon adapted however and did well in all her courses, graduating from Lincoln High School in 1934.

Nellie Wilson

"When I was a teenager, any black person who set a goal for himself and was lucky enough to achieve that goal was just that — lucky," Nellie commented. Most blacks — men and women — were relegated to menial work. Nellie was aware of only a few black people in the professions. One of them was a local nurse who became her role model. But Nellie's hopes for entering a nursing school were dashed when, during a special "Career Day" in high school, the announcement was made: "If there are any Negro girls here,

> *"When I was a teenager, any black person who set a goal for himself and was lucky enough to achieve that goal was just that — lucky."*

you may as well go back to your homerooms right now because there is no medical facility in the state of Wisconsin that will accept Negro girls as students." "So there it was," said Nellie, "What do you do?"

Adding to the burden of racism in finding a job was the fact that Nellie graduated and began searching for work in the depths of the Depression. "I did all sorts of things for an honest living," she said, "but it was always menial, undesirable work, cleaning up — that's all there was." She spent a year working for a family in Nashotah. It was a domestic live-in situation in which she was "at their beck and call 24 hours a day." For this, Nellie said, "She paid me the magnificent sum of $3.25 per week." When Nellie complained after working there a year, her wages were raised to just $3.50.

Nellie quit the job in Nashotah and returned to Milwaukee, where she had begun seeing her future husband, Alvin Wilson. They married in 1935 and had two daughters — Eleanor, born in 1937, and Norma Estelle or Stella, born in 1939. But the economic hard times took a toll on her marriage. The couple separated, and Nellie was soon on her own and responsible for the care of two children. "It was hard, really, really hard," she said. Once, she responded to a call for lunchroom work in the public schools. She took the civil service exam and knew she did well, but was assigned to cleaning the floors at City Hall. "I was so glad when I got to A.O. Smith," she said.

Like Our Sisters Before Us

Prior to World War II, A.O. Smith hired no African Americans and blacks walking near the plant were likely to be spit on by workers, according to Nellie. But all this changed with the war and the passage of the Fair Employment Practices Act, which required defense contractors to hire blacks. Civil rights leader A. Phillip Randolph had threatened President Roosevelt with a march of thousands of Negroes on Washington if they were not given the opportunity to work in the expanding defense industries. "As a result of that threat," said Nellie, "I got into A.O. Smith's."

"Once [African Americans] got in there, there was a kind of brotherhood and camaraderie in the country those days because we had to win the war. That's all there was to it, and so labor was necessary and the more skilled you were, the more important you were.... When the war was over, most folks went back to things as usual, the way they were before. It was quite a letdown. But while [the war] was going, we were 100% Americans."

A.O. Smith sent Nellie to a six-week training course which prepared her for her first job there. It required skill and accuracy. "Since I had a good math background, I ended up in a pretty decent job doing precision inspection on airplane propellers, working with the precision instruments and reading blueprints. I liked it. I remember asking my boss if I was doing the job alright. He asked me: 'Are you doing the best you can?' I said, 'I'm doing the best I can.' He said, 'Well, if you're doing the best you can, that's all anybody can do,' and from then on I had confidence."

The first union person Nellie met was a steward who talked her into joining the union: "He told me about all the benefits the union had, and I couldn't believe every time I looked around I had another check, back pay for something, or an increase in pay. You had job security — nobody could just come in and fire you — and all these good things. He said, 'You ought to want to be a part of keeping something like that going.' I agreed with him and I joined the union. I was all gung-ho."

Nellie didn't become deeply involved in the union until many years later, however. She worked long hours during the war and spent what free time she had with her children. A neighborhood woman known as "Miss Sadie" cared for the girls while Nellie worked. Nellie recalled the arrangement as almost ideal: "Miss Sadie had never had

Nellie Wilson

children and they met a need in her life, and they respected her because they knew she would get hold of their butts if they didn't mind!"

When the war ended, A.O. Smith laid off many workers, and the first to go were the women. "That's where the union came in 100%," Nellie said. "The company did not want us there, period. We insisted that the company recall [women] after World War II because [they] were our members. We knew that kind of work in there was not the kind of work a woman

Young Nellie Wilson

should be doing, but the company has an obligation to call you back. If you can't handle it, you quit. But they must give you a chance."

After the war, A.O. Smith shifted from the diverse needs of military contracts to automotive production, which many workers found more challenging. "Women went out of there by the hundreds," Nellie said, "but some of us stayed. [The work] was man-killing, awful. There was the heavy lifting, the dirt, the noise, the grease, the speed, everything undesirable, but the money was good. One foreman used to say, 'If the women ain't got brains enough to quit we'll kill 'em, and they damn near did, too. It was awful. But I had those girls to educate. From Day 1, we made the same amount of money that the men made." Making the work even more difficult for the women were the taunts of their male co-workers: "You're getting a man's pay, you're supposed to be able to do a man's work!" Many women gave up, Nellie said, but those who stayed on stuck together and got tough.

Through the 1950's, Nellie worked on the assembly line and then as a punch press operator. Co-workers who had observed Nellie confronting the foreman on rates suggested that she run for the job of steward. Nellie recalled that they put it to her in this way: "Every time we get a steward, a good steward, the company either buys them off or promotes them to being a temporary supervisor. And we figured that you being a black woman, they ain't gonna do either one for you."

"Can you believe it?" Nellie asked. "That's how I got to be a steward in the first place. When [the company] started their buying-off tactics, I said 'I don't need it.' I kept right on bitchin', kept right on fighting grievances...." Realizing they couldn't buy her off, the company eventually squeezed her out, transferring her to second shift after a temporary layoff. This move meant she lost her steward position. "But that didn't stop me," Nellie said with satisfaction, "I was still a thorn in their side."

"After I got to be a steward, we had an agreement. If the industrial engineer came out and set a rate, that's what the rate would be, today, tomorrow, forevermore, unless something is changed. If it's a good rate, we'll work it. If it's a poor rate, we'll grieve it. And

Nellie Wilson and fellow members of Smith Steelworkers Local 19806 at the School for Workers in Madison, early 1960's

Nellie Wilson

we did grieve it — over and over again. I filed so many grievances. My grievances were all about money, incentive rates and money." At the time she was steward, Nellie took classes at the University of Wisconsin Extension School for Workers in Madison. From the knowledge she gained there in time-study courses, she was able to come back to A.O. Smith and clock various machines, determining discrepancies in their speeds and outputs that had the effect of cheating workers.

"The hardest job I had being a steward or even an officer was to listen to somebody's complaint, go and read the contract and get back to him and tell him, 'According to article so-and-so, section so-and-so, you don't have anything coming,' — and still keep his friendship. That was the hardest thing to do."

In 1963, Nellie attended the March on Washington which featured the "I Have a Dream" address of Dr. Martin Luther King, Jr. She was visiting friends in San Antonio when she saw publicity about the civil rights march and decided to go: "I just thought of all the times I might have been promoted or the jobs I might have had had I not been black." She called it "the most breathtaking spectacle I've ever seen in my life. I don't expect to ever see anything like that again. Two hundred and fifty thousand people is an awful lot of people. What a power that man had to galvanize that many people nonviolently! ...I was glad to be a part of it."

"I came back fired up. There was definitely a commitment around A.O. Smith to do something. At that time, I ended up being part of a group that included the presidents of big corporations in Milwaukee who used to meet down at the labor council's offices. The idea was to discuss 'What can we do to alleviate the situation?' There was hope in the air. Everybody was rushing to do what we could."

Nellie was appointed to various boards and commissions in the 1960's and '70's, among them the Milwaukee chapter of the Red Cross, the Children's Service Society, the Apprenticeship Advisory Council and the State Personnel Board. She believes many of these appointments were the direct result of the civil rights movement, which caused many organizations to search for black representatives. "Boy, I was integrating all over — everywhere!" Nellie joked. "They were following the leader by getting a black to put in the window — except I had a lot more to do than sit up in the window."

Shortly after her return from Washington, Nellie, encouraged by some union brothers and her good friend, Helen Hensler, decided to run for a seat on the Executive Board of Local 19806. She launched a spirited campaign whose slogan was "In unity there is strength." She had her photo placed on cards which supporters distributed throughout the plant. Nellie won the primary and then worked successfully for the additional votes needed to win the final run-off. "Oh, it was thrilling!" she said of the victory. "I won the first time around and then I didn't stop winning."

Her victory was indeed significant because very few individuals running the first time ever won office, and Nellie was the first African American woman to sit on the Executive Board of Local 19806. She served on the board until her retirement in 1969. During most of those years, she was the sole woman on the board, serving with eleven men.

> *"An issue would come up and I'd state my opinion and they'd say, 'Well, that's pretty good for a woman.'"*

Nellie proved to be as diligent an officer as she had been a steward. But even on the Executive Board she was still subject to the sexist attitudes of the men around her: "An issue would come up and I'd state my opinion and they'd say, 'Well, that's pretty good for a woman.'"

Nellie's proudest contribution while on the Board of Local 19806 was her championing of Clara Streicher's grievance which ended occupational barriers against women throughout A.O. Smith. "It was a clear case of the company denying a woman a job because she was a woman," Nellie declared. "If she'd been a man, she would have had that job. I had seen enough of that and experienced enough of that around A.O. Smith's myself." The union's attorneys advised the board not to send Clara's complaint to arbitration, but Nellie was persistent: "I just kept up like a broken record, 'But if she'd have been a man she'd have the job.' I lobbied each member of the Executive Board individually. They finally took the case to arbitration, the union won, Clara got a whole bunch of back pay, and anything that you wanted to be you could be from then on because of Clara Streicher's case."

The lack of women in apprenticeships also infuriated Nellie ("The apprenticeship system was the purview of males, period! There were no women electricians, no women millwrights. All the industrial apprenticeships — none of them had any women!"), so she worked in several capacities to bring about change: in her communications with leaders of the building trades while on the Milwaukee County Labor Council; in her position on the state's Apprenticeship Advisory Council; and through job and training placements with the Human Resource Development Institute (HRDI).

During the height of her union activism in the 1960's, Nellie decided to go back to school, "at first, to see if I was capable of learning anything at my age" and then to acquire skills that might land her a future job outside the factory. She earned a bachelor's degree in Social Welfare from the University of Wisconsin-Milwaukee and completed the course work for a master's degree in Urban Affairs. She came "a long way," she mused, from that one-room schoolhouse in Texas.

Nellie, who was getting tired of shop work, retired from A.O. Smith in 1969. She worked for a year with the Midwest Office of Economic Opportunity Labor Leadership Project, which trained union members to become effective advocates for the poor in their communities. She gained valuable experience in administrative work and public speaking. She then settled in to an 11-year stint as area representative with the Human Resources Development Institute, where the job was a good match for a person of Nellie's experience and social commitment.

"I guess my most rewarding experience came after I got to HRDI," said Nellie, "where the job was finding jobs for hard-core disadvantaged people, which went on to include Vietnam-era veterans, women in non-traditional jobs, ex-offenders, even to professional people. It was through direct job placement. It was through training programs. It was through the apprenticeship system." The key was learning about job openings from labor councils throughout the state and developing relationships with personnel managers at many businesses. "We did better putting people in union shops than the Job Service did. It was a really good program."

Nellie recalled fondly one Easter morning when three young women appeared at her door offering her flowers. They identified themselves as women she had placed in good jobs at Harley-Davidson, and they had just stopped by to show their appreciation. "When you know that you're the bridge that takes somebody over, that's a really good feeling," said Nellie.

> *"There were so many things I could not do or do with reservations because I was a woman. ...If you don't turn feminist, something's got to be wrong with you!"*

Unfortunately, the HRDI depended on federal funds for the job placement service, and when President Reagan ended the Comprehensive Employment and Training Act in the early 1980's, Nellie's job with the HRDI came to a close. Nellie, then 65 years old, decided to retire permanently. She remained active with numerous groups, including the Urban League, the Coalition of Labor Union Women and the American Association of Retired Persons, serving as a spokesperson for the AARP's Minority Affairs Initiative.

Looking back on her work life, Nellie paid tribute to some of the "top-notch" individuals who helped her along the way: Aaron Tolliver and Bob Durkin at Local 19806; Helen Hensler in the A.O. Smith office; Virginia Hart at the School for Workers; and Catherine Conroy on the Executive Board of the State AFL-CIO.

Nellie expressed grave concern about the beating the labor movement has taken since the 1980's. She cited Reagan's union-busting legacy, legislative changes that benefit business at labor's expense, management's use of anti-union attorneys and consultants, the flow of jobs outside the US, and the fact that union workers no longer vote as a block for their own interests. All these are major challenges for which the new generation of unionists must find creative solutions.

When asked if she considers herself a feminist, Nellie's heartfelt reply reflected her lifetime experience. She said she was asked the same question by an AFL-CIO official when she applied for the job

Nellie Wilson

at the HRDI, "and I'm gonna tell you what I told him. I told him, 'I was one of the ones that helped start the goddam thing!' That's what I told him, because I had been fighting for a long time, first one thing and then another you can't do because there's all this b.s. that goes along with 'but you are a woman.'"

"I can never forget how long it took to get credit cards in my name without someone asking me about 'mister.' It just made you feel like you were almost a person but not quite. The same thing with renting houses. 'Where is your husband?' What's husband got to do with it? From Day 1 when I found myself with the children I found there were so many things I could not do or do with reservations because I was a woman. I started resenting the fact that I was subjected to that kind of treatment. By the time you get your face washed with that once a week and you're taking care of the man's responsibilities, if you don't turn feminist, something's got to be wrong with you! That's why I say I got started long before the movement got started. I couldn't be anything different."

Nellie Wilson, 1989

DORIS THOM

*"I was a fighter then,
and I think I'd be a fighter again."*

Looking back on her years as a pioneering woman unionist, a thoughtful Doris Thom commented that she is "very definitely" a feminist. "I've had to fight for nearly everything I've ever wanted.... If you hadn't pushed back, you would have accepted what you were offered, and I wasn't willing to do that."

Doris achieved several important "firsts" for women while employed by General Motors' Fisher Body Plant in Janesville between 1955-69. When Doris was denied a transfer from the cushion line to the all-male trim department, her successful grievance helped open all of the plant's jobs to women. Doris became the first female committeewoman in 1960 and, as recording secretary from 1961-68, was the first woman to sit on the Executive Board of UAW Local 95. She was an active member of the UAW Region 10 Women's Committee and, after her retirement, served on the Governor's Commission on the Status of Women.

Doris was born on March 8, 1920 at her family homestead in Janesville. She was the youngest of three girls and three boys born to Albert and Alvina Schumacher, whose own parents had immigrated from Germany. Albert was a switchman for the Chicago &

Doris Thom

Northwestern Railroad — a "strong union man" according to Doris, who recalled him selling tickets to union events and taking the family to union-sponsored picnics.

But the death of her father in a work-related accident when she was just ten years old shook her family and gave Doris an early lesson in the insensitivities of companies, who, she noted, can sometimes behave like "little gods." The C&NW railroad offered Alvina Schumacher a lifetime pass as compensation for the death of her husband, but she declined, saying, "No, they owe me my husband's life and his livelihood." Mrs. Schumacher held out for a financial settlement which enabled

Little Doris Schumacher

her to support her six children during the difficult years of the Depression.

"It wasn't until later years when I realized just exactly what she had done and what an accomplishment it was," Doris said of her mother. "At that time, women were just not the fighters, I don't think, that they are now. They sort of went along with most things. I give her an awfully lot of credit for not being the kind that sat back and said, 'Alright, I'll take what you give me.' ...My mother was a strong woman — apparently that's where I get it."

Except for the loss of her father, Doris recalled her childhood and teen years as mostly happy. She did well in school and excelled in sports, playing on softball, hockey and basketball teams. She enjoyed tennis and skating as well. She played a lot with her youngest brother and other boys and learned "to be as tough as the rest of them." But she was also aware of the limitations placed on girls. Doris still regrets

Like Our Sisters Before Us

that after graduation from Janesville High School there were no scholarships available to her as a woman who wanted to pursue athletics in college.

On New Year's Eve 1938, Doris married Henry "Hank" Thom, a boy who had lived just four blocks away. "I saw him ice-skating and I kind of liked his looks," she said of Hank. They had three children together: Don, Paul, and Patty. Hank worked at the Rock River Woolen Mill for almost 15 years. He developed emphysema from his many years of stamping oily wool in confined quarters with few if any safety or health precautions. Only afterwards did he realize the impact this had on his health. He left the mill to work at General Motors where he could make more money. Doris and Hank spent more than 55 happy years together until lung disease took Hank's life in 1994.

Doris's first job in 1940-41 was at the Parker Pen Co. repairing nibs on pens. "It was kind of an eye opener for me because I had never been out of the home working before then," she said. "I enjoyed the people." Doris can't remember if there was a union at Parker, though the pay seemed good — "being my first job I thought it was wonderful." But there were no regular break times and she recalled having to raise her hand to be excused for the restroom. Grandmother Thom looked after baby Don while Doris worked.

Her motive in seeking employment outside the home? "Economics. You bet — we needed the money. We were like every other young family. We wanted a home of our own. That was the objective." Doris and Hank also wanted to save money to ensure that their children "had the education that we weren't able to get."

After a year at Parker Pen, Doris was laid off, but she soon found employment at Gilman Engineering, whose workers built emergency landing gear for the Grumman Hellcat fighter. "The war was on. The fellows were gone. They needed people to do their work but they hesitated a long time [about hiring women]," Doris recalled. The first group of women "worked out so successfully, they decided to hire more, and I was in the second group [of women] to come in."

After awhile, Doris and other women workers began asking why they couldn't do the things men did, like sharpening their own tools and grinding wheels. At first the foremen — all male — were "overjoyed" the women were willing to take on more tasks. But when they then asked for commensurate pay, Doris said, "Boom! The next

Doris Thom

day the order went out: 'Women will no longer touch any kind of tools. They will not dress their grinding wheels. They will only do what the foreman tells them to do.' ...They wanted to be sure that when the fellows came back from service, there weren't women engineers in the plant."

At this point Doris sought out the union, Machinists Local 1266. "If I'm gonna be part of something, I want to know how it works, what's going on," she said. "I was an oddity at first. I mean I was a woman and I was coming [to union meetings], and *what was I doing there?*" She began by listening carefully and asking questions. In a short time, she was elected recording secretary. But even her position as a union officer could not save her job when she became pregnant with her second child. In those days, pregnancy meant automatic termination. "Past practice" was cited as the rationale, and Doris admits she did not challenge it at the time. The next years were spent raising her children and establishing a secure home for the family.

> **"They wanted to be sure that when the fellows came back from service, there weren't women engineers in the plant."**

Doris worked seasonal jobs in the early 1950's. These included pelting mink at the MacFarlane Mink Ranch — "difficult work, hard on the wrists" — and plucking turkeys — "messy job" — at the Blackhawk Hatchery. She heard about openings at the General Motors plant from her brother Albert, who was active in the union there. He actually discouraged her from applying, saying that she "didn't belong there." But Doris, determined to improve her family's financial standing, applied and began work on the cushion line April 5, 1955.

The cushion line was a segregated area, and with the exception of the foremen and relief men, it was staffed entirely by women. Doris's first job was "hog-ringing," jump-gun work putting clips on the cushions to attach them to the metal frame. "It was not easy work. It was difficult work," she remembered. She began to observe other jobs: "Most of them looked easier than what we [women] were doing and I wondered why."

Like Our Sisters Before Us

Doris had joined Local 95 of the United Auto Workers immediately upon starting at General Motors. In 1960, she decided to run for alternate committeeman, a position akin to being a steward. She was voted in by her colleagues on the cushion line. At first it was "a big joke," she said, that a woman had gained such a position, but the laughing turned to grudging respect when she won the first grievance on behalf of a worker. Empowered by her new role, she soon embarked on a successful campaign for recording secretary of Local 95, becoming the first woman to sit on its 18-member Executive Board.

As an officer, Doris recalls "learning, learning all the time." In the summers, she attended the School for Workers at the University of Wisconsin, where she took courses in grievance procedures, union management and political organizing. Doris also attended UAW Region 10 Women's Committee meetings in Milwaukee and a UAW national convention. Through her exposure to other union sisters, Doris discovered that women in other plants were not restricted to the cushion line but worked at a variety of jobs. At about the time that Congress was adopting the Equal Pay Act (1963) and the Civil Rights Act (1964), which prohibited job discrimination against women, Doris was increasingly questioning the limits on women's opportunities at the GM plant in Janesville. Noting that many jobs looked less demanding than her duties on the cushion line, Doris tried to apply for transfers to other jobs. But company managers refused to accept her applications.

> *"All I heard was, 'This is past practice. We do not have women going out of the cushion line.'"*

In July 1965, Doris filed a grievance and sent a copy of it to the Wisconsin Industrial Commission and to the federal Equal Employment Opportunity Commission. Shortly afterward, an investigator from the state came to Janesville to look into the matter. He told Doris he could find no records that she had ever applied for different jobs. "Well, of course you didn't," she told him, "because

Doris Thom

I was not allowed to sign anything. They would not accept my application for signing up. All I heard was, 'This is past practice. We do not have women going out of the cushion line.'" The official investigated further and concluded that Doris had a legitimate case.

A few weeks later, "GM flew in two of their lawyers and I sat down with all my Executive Board again, with Lou Atkins from the Region 10 office, and Bob Vicars, who was chairman. And Lou, in his way, said: 'Young lady, I hope you know what you're doing.' I said, 'You bet I do.' Then one of the lawyers said: 'Well, it's going to mean changing all [GM's] books and all [their] flow charts.' And I said 'Fine.' That's all. There was nothing more said...because apparently they were told right then and there: 'You are going against the law now. The law has been passed. This woman has the right to do what she's asking to do.' And that was the end of it. That was the end of it but that was the beginning of it."

"So, I had the law on my side but I couldn't get the jobs. I went in and signed up for every job that was available — anything that I saw that I knew that I could do. But I found that the foremen were going up and down the lines telling the men 'Do you want a woman working on your line? If you don't, you'd better get down and sign up for that job. You have more seniority than she does.' And by this time, I had almost ten years seniority."

Doris went in to see the plant manager to insist that he rein in the foremen. She let him know she would not hesitate to bring another complaint to the commission and reminded him that he could be fined up to $10,000 a day for denying her access to different jobs. He assured her he was unaware of the attempts to block her efforts, but would see that they stopped. That seemed to do the trick because the harassment ended and she soon won her transfer.

"My first job was working in a pit putting on weatherstripping in the middle of the plant. I had people coming from every direction looking down [at me] like a monkey in a cage, you know. [They would] point: 'There's a woman down there!' And I would work, keep on working. And of course it was terrible. It was just awful. You can't imagine. Working in a place where the women couldn't get to you because they couldn't take that long a relief time. So nobody could back you up or give you a little encouragement. Nobody would talk to you. The only people that would talk at all would be the relief person.

Like Our Sisters Before Us

'There's a woman and, doggone it, who does she think she is coming down here and taking our jobs?' ...It was such a definite feeling — hostility. I used to go home nights and think, 'I don't have to go back there, I don't have to take this kind of thing.' And then I'd think: 'Yes, you do. You started this and you're going to finish it.'"

Doris finally won their hearts through their stomachs. "Factory workers are chow hounds," she noted, "and on birthdays people usually brought treats. So I brought in a chocolate cake and a white cake. I brought in paper plates and plastic forks, and I sent word along with a relief man that 'It's my birthday, and I would like to have people come and have a piece of my birthday cake. Tell them they'll be right here where I work and if they'd like a piece to come and get it.' Before the end of the shift was over I think that everyone up and down the line had been there.... And that was it, that broke the ice."

Her next battle was over restroom facilities. The time it took Doris to walk to and from the women's room was longer than her relief time. She told her committeeman: "'Either I've got to have a restroom of my own or I've got to go in the restroom with the men or

Doris Thom, 1990

you're going to have to give me more time.' They took it to grievance and, of course, they couldn't put up a restroom for one woman, and I kept saying, 'You know, there isn't always going to be only one woman. We're going to have more, believe me.' So it was quickly resolved. I was given more time and believe me, I took it."

"I couldn't have made it through this without the support of my family. They went through tough times, too. The kids remember getting threatening calls at home while I worked the night shift. The callers said that I should get back to the cushion line where I belonged. And it wasn't easy for Hank either, because he also worked at the plant and would get guff from fellow workers. Yet he always encouraged me and supported my decisions. He also helped out at home while I worked. We truly raised our kids together."

But Doris still felt like "I was damned if I did and damned if I didn't." Despite the fact that she was paving the way for them, many women in the plant did not initially support her.

"The women were very unhappy — some of them — because I had made that change. The talk had gone out through the plant that now women are going to start losing their jobs. They're going to put you on a job somewhere and you're not going to be able to do it and out the door you're going because there's nothing else for you to do. I managed to get down there a couple of times and talk to some of them and say 'That's not true. They cannot put you out.' 'Well what if we're too small to do some of these jobs?' I said: 'Then don't apply for them. Stay in the cushion line if you're happier here. But look what I'm making over what you're making now.' And, gradually, they began to see it."

The full impact of her stand for women's rights only became apparent a few years later, at the time Doris retired from GM in 1969. "At that time you were seeing women all over the plant in many, many areas, in all different kinds of work, and they were then beginning to realize what was happening."

Doris serves as cushion line reunion chairperson, and at a recent reunion someone noted that "If it weren't for Doris, we wouldn't be all over the plant." Everyone applauded and gave her a standing ovation. "It was so good to see that happen, because for so many years you felt like you were kind of — you know," Doris trailed off. "At the time, you weren't too pleased even with yourself because you wondered if what you were doing was really right." Doris doesn't wonder any more.

Looking back, Doris noted that union activism unquestionably increased her self-confidence and that, as a white woman in a mostly white town, working with and befriending black people helped her to overcome her prejudices.

In addition to her union involvement, Doris has always been active in her community. She was a founder of the Blackhawk Credit Union in 1965. She served as president of Rock County Democratic Women for 15 years, and credited the UAW Region 10 Women's Committee with being the "foot soldiers" in the successful political campaigns of John Kennedy, Gaylord Nelson, and many others. She also served on the Governor's Commission on the Status of Women from 1971 to 1975, lending her experience as a working woman and union activist to the organization which advocated for women's rights in the home, community and workplace. Doris returned to UAW Local 95 when she was invited to become a member of its women's committee in 1995.

Asked if there was anything about her work life she would do differently, Doris responded: "I don't think so. I was a fighter then, and I think I'd be a fighter again."

LEE SCHMELING

*"We didn't go around raising hell.
We just wanted to make sure
we could protect our rights."*

⎯⎯⎯⎯⎯⎯⎯⎯⎯⎯

Lee Schmeling was something of a late bloomer when it came to the labor movement. She worked at the George Banta Company in Menasha for eleven years before joining the union there. "I knew there was a union, but there was really nobody pushing it," she recalled. "I guess most of us never really thought about it. I mean, after all, what did the union do for me?"

Lee underwent a remarkable transformation, however, becoming the very first woman president of Local 32B of the International Brotherhood of Bookbinders, representing hundreds of workers at the Banta Company. She played a leading role in the 1977 strike against Banta and served from 1979-1992 as president of Local 382 and, later, Local 77P, which resulted from a merger of bookbinders and lithographers under the auspices of the Graphic Arts International Union (GAIU), now the Graphic Communications International Union (GCIU). Lee became a board member of GAIU, served for many years on the Fox Valley Area Labor Council, and contributed her expertise as a labor representative on the Advisory Board of the Wisconsin Youth Apprenticeship Program.

Like Our Sisters Before Us

Lee was born in High Cliff, Wisconsin on August 5, 1932 and was raised on a farm with her four sisters and cousins. Her father, Otto Schmeling, got a union job with the American Can Company and was able to buy a house for the family in Neenah. Lee attended High Cliff Elementary School and then Neenah High School. "I didn't have time to play around in school because my mother was sick a lot and I came home to help with the kids," Lee said. When her mother, Elsie, died, Lee took over more household responsibilities and became a mother figure. "I didn't mind that. I'm almost like their parent and I just love it," she said of her siblings and cousins. "I look at it as a blessing because we're a real close family."

After Lee graduated from Neenah High School, her very first job was as a cab driver — the only female cabbie in Neenah-Menasha. She never felt put down or harassed in that position, "Don't ask me why," she said incredulously. "I don't know if it's something I generate, but it's never, never been an issue."

In 1951, she began work at Banta, one of the largest printers in the US, where she worked as an "inserter," feeding books into a stitcher. Because no one was "pushing it," Lee didn't join the union until 1962. But she made up for lost time by becoming deeply involved in union activities very quickly.

It began one day when she was approached by Ambrose "Amby" Magalski, president of Local 32B (Bookbinders). "He just came to me one day and he said, 'Lee, I got kids at home and I don't have time to be the president. I want you to join the union. First, you'll be my steward and then you're gonna take my place.' I said, 'Okay, alright, where do I have to go?' I went over to the hall, I joined the union and he said, 'You're the steward.' That was it. I was suddenly a steward. Can you believe it?"

Magalski sent Lee to steward training classes taught at the University of Wisconsin Extension School for Workers. The classes "opened up a whole new world for me," she said. An avid student, Lee immediately shared the information she gained with others in her local: "I set up in my own basement a training from what I had learned. I took it and converted it for them to learn. We even made up small certificates when they finished."

"The grievances we got were pretty legitimate," Lee commented, "unless you had some new people and they didn't understand; then we'd explain it to them. I really have, I believe, great credibility. Because if I think you're wrong what I'll do is listen to you, and then I'll walk you through it from my perspective. I've never said no to a grievance, but I'll also tell them that 'you're making a mistake.' I'm not afraid of grievances, but I don't like running with something that has no merit." Most grievances, she said, were resolved in a timely manner.

A complaint that Lee herself filed had the happy effect of ensuring that all jobs at the Banta Company were henceforth open to qualified women. The year was 1966, and by this time Lee had been elected president of her local, a part-time position. Lee was still working as an inserter, but saw a posting for a trainee machine operator, a job which, to that point, had always been filled by men.

"We had a new guy — three months off the street. The company gave it to him, and I said, 'Wait a minute, the Equal Employment Opportunity Commission says anybody can sign for it,' and they refused to give it to me, even though I had more experience and seniority. So I filed a charge [with the Wisconsin Industrial Commission]. The International was even angry with me because at that time I was president of the union. I said, 'Well, then I'll resign, but *I am gonna file it.'* ...It didn't take long before we got a decision back that said, 'Yes,' I was entitled to the job." The Industrial Commission supported her claim, Banta issued a policy forbidding such bias, and Lee was given the job as trainee machine operator.

> *"It didn't take long before we got a decision back that said, 'Yes,' I was entitled to the job."*

She'll never forget how "the boss took me over to the machine [and said]: 'There's a red button, you stop it. With this green one you turn it on. *You wanted to run it, now run it!'* One of the guys made a snide remark about taking [the men's] high-paid jobs, but a machine operator said: 'If she's good enough to represent us, she's good enough to work with us.' And that was it. We never had discrimination again at the Banta Company. It just fell right into place."

In 1976, Lee became full-time president of Local 32B and was soon presented with her greatest challenge. The Banta Company demanded concessions from its workers in the new contract being negotiated. These concessions included increased hours, cuts in workers' cost-of-living allowances and insurance coverage, and the revocation of the union security clause. "There was no way to avert it," Lee said about the strike. "The company dug in, and we just wouldn't give it up."

On April 4, 1977, after rejecting their proposed contract, 750 members of Locals 32B and 88L (Lithographers) walked off the job. The strike lasted a grueling six months. There were tense picket lines and confrontations with strikebreakers and Wackenhut guards hired by Banta. Outfitted with helmets, clubs and large shields, the Wackenhuts presented an intimidating front which strikers did their best to deflate through jokes and taunts. Lee was in the thick of it, being saved by a fellow striker from a billy club blow one day and being charged with obstructing police for her picketing tactics another. Police arrested more than 60 people, but most of the charges were later dropped. High points of the strike for Lee were the solidarity displayed by the Fox Valley Area Labor Council, the coordinating body for local unions, and the one-day shutdown of the Banta Company's US plants by picketers.

"My local was not involved with the labor council," Lee explained. "But [Fox Valley Area Labor Council President] Mike Paul came to me and he said, 'Lee, we'd like to put on a car cavalcade for your people because they're on strike. Would you like that?' I said, 'I would.' Well, there were *hundreds* of cars and trucks. They closed off all of Neenah-Menasha! They went around the Banta Company in a great big circle — 500 cars. We've never seen anything like it before or since."

"We happen to have four or five Banta subsidiaries in Ohio and Minnesota. One morning I was really ticked because I was missing all my pickets. But at 7:05 I got a call from the company that every corporation was shut down because there were pickets there. We moved them in at night and in the morning we shut the whole corporation down in the United States! The guys loved it. But the company called me to say, 'You've got pickets over there. Don't you know you can't do that?' And I said, '*What?!* My God, no. I was

Lee Schmeling

Local 32B President Lee Schmeling in action during the 1977 strike against Banta. (Neenah-Menasha Daily Northwestern photo)

wondering what happened. It was so foggy last night they must have gotten lost.'"

Neither federal mediation nor intervention by International union representatives could budge Banta from its hard line. Toward the end, with workers beginning to cross picket lines, the lithographers reluctantly voted to accept the company's offer. It was a particularly painful situation for Lee, who ended up advising her own members to vote for the contract. Rejecting it would have "broken the union," she reasoned, though accepting it, she acknowledged, ushered in the beginning of the "take-away cycle."

In the wake of the strike, Locals 32B and 88L, merged. "We decided that in order to survive, we would have to merge our two unions," Lee said. This came about in April of 1978, and Lee was elected president of the newly created Local 382. "I thought it would be a problem for all the pressmen and prep people to adjust to, but there was really nothing you could call a growing pain," Lee commented. "It just worked out. It was a blessing."

Like Our Sisters Before Us

Almost ten years after the strike, Local 382 won a $2 million settlement from Banta. It was compensation for striking workers who were not recalled by the company for up to one year or more after the strike ended. Local 382 filed an unfair labor practices complaint which was upheld by the National Labor Relations Board. The settlement, which Lee called "a big victory," resulted from that ruling.

Automation displaced many Banta workers over the years. According to Lee, in January 1976, there were about 900 workers at Banta. In the mid-1990's there were less than 400. "Automation has done most of that," she said. "And a lot of the handwork and tablework has been sent to non-union workers around the valley."

Lee felt her primary duty as union president was to ensure that her members had a future. One of her proudest achievements, therefore, was the establishment of on-site education and training programs at Banta.

"This way," she said, "you have no excuse to tell me that you can't train to run a piece of equipment, because if you've got a problem reading, [with] computers, math, you can come right over

In 1993, Lee Schmeling poses with a photo of the Wackenhut squads sent in to intimidate strikers in 1977.

here and get all the training you need. To me, that's been one of the biggest breakthroughs. With the training you've got from the time you walk in that door, you have every opportunity to take every bit of it. You can retire from that high-skill, high-paid job without being removed from it someplace along the way, because you've got everything made available to you now."

Another of Lee's "biggest cares and loves" has been advocacy on behalf of handicapped people both inside and outside of work. She supported tailoring jobs and job spaces to the needs of disabled workers and met with area school boards to advise them about preparing children with special needs for future jobs. Well-versed in the provisions of the Americans with Disabilities Act, she was often consulted for advice on its implementation.

Did she have any regrets about her union activism? "If I had to do it over, when I became the president of the union I would have supported membership in the labor council. It's a shame that my local all those years sat back. You didn't realize the importance of it. I don't think I really did until we got into that strike, because we thought we were so big. We thought we were 900 people. We didn't have to worry. The company was always good to us. But it was shown to me that you can be 900 people and it doesn't mean nothing. If they want to crush you, they'll crush you."

Lee credited the labor council with widening her perspective and spurring her involvement in other areas of workplace concern, including education and youth apprenticeship. "There's no way I would be doing them if the labor council hadn't opened the doors," she said. "They're not being done just for my local. They're being done for the labor movement. I take great pride in our labor council. I really do. There are so many talented people that have ideas and share them with you. I think they are doing a tremendous job."

"You know, we don't publicize all the good we do. We're weak on that. It's rare you ever read about it. It's rare that you ever hear or see it on TV. The only time [the public] hear[s] about us is when we have a strike or when we do something wrong."

"I know that we can't change the world overnight, but I know that if we keep plugging away...." Lee trailed off hopefully. "We didn't go around raising hell. We just wanted to make sure we could protect our rights."

HELEN HENSLER

"Men are not going to do it for us.
We have to learn how to play the game. "

Why in the world would 74-year-old Helen Hensler give up her retirement and take on the strenuous job of business representative for her financially strapped office workers' local? "I felt that I owed my union for providing 55 years of good wages, full health insurance coverage, excellent pension coverage, job security and a means for addressing any grievances that would arise," Helen said. "This was a way I could repay Local 9 in some small way for providing me with the good life I have enjoyed all these years."

Helen Hensler showed this kind of dedication throughout her long union career. She was an active member and then business representative of the Office and Professional Employees International Union (OPEIU) Local 9 in Milwaukee from 1939 until her retirement in 1997. She was first a steward, then recording secretary (1952-75) and, finally, president of Local 9 (1975-79). Women's rights were a central focus of her union career. Helen was a founder of the Wisconsin AFL-CIO Women's Committee, a founder and officer of the Coalition of Labor Union Women, a member of the Governor's Commission on the Status of Women (1971-79), and a delegate to the Milwaukee County Labor Council for several decades.

Helen Hensler

Helen was the first of four daughters born to Otto Hensler and Helen Domres Hensler on July 22, 1919 in Milwaukee. Mrs. Hensler worked briefly at a laundry but gave her full attention to child care as her daughters were born. Mr. Hensler worked seven days a week up to ten hours a day as a milkman for the Gridley Dairy Company (later, Borden's), where an organizing campaign by the Teamsters led to a "very bitter strike which made a great impression on me," Helen said.

"In 1934, when the Teamsters tried to organize Gridley, [my father] became very active in helping to push for the union there. He believed strongly in it. One of the main reasons was job security. Of course, the wages were terrible too. They just felt they were entitled to more," Helen recalled. The strike dragged on for several months and became violent, with milk wagons overturned. "He kept on telling us that unless they won [the union], there wouldn't be a better life for us. I recall during that time my folks talking about how

> *"After they got the union, things were better for the workers and for us as a family."*

tough things were, but somehow or other, they squeaked through. My mother was very supportive. She told us, 'The only way to gain anything is to make a few sacrifices in life. You'll see, this is going to pay off.'"

"After they got the union, things *were* better for the workers and for us as a family," Helen said. Her father got a pay raise and was given one day off per week. He also became eligible for paid vacations and a pension. One day several years later, Helen asked her father about rumors she had heard of gangsters in the Teamsters' union. "Young lady," he replied sternly, "if it wasn't for those Teamsters, you wouldn't be sitting in the position that you are today." "He was a very loyal union member," Helen said, "and I'm the same way."

After the death of her mother in childbirth, Helen, at age 16, was forced to assume greater family responsibilities. Chief among these was looking after her three sisters, the youngest of whom was just four years old. Arrangements were made for Helen to spend half-days at Washington High School so she could look after her sisters. Her father, she said, "made up his mind that this family was going to stay together — and we did. We're a close family. We're all independent and we're spread out a little now, but we're still pretty close and we help each other out when the need arises."

"I was a good student," Helen said of her high school years. "I liked school and things came rather easy for me." She graduated one semester after her class due to her family responsibilities. She would like to have gone on to college but "the money just wasn't there" to pay for it. Instead, she began to look for work, a challenge while the Depression was still on. "I always liked office work," she said, "and I thought I'd like to be a secretary for the president or vice-president of some big company."

Helen Hensler, 1933

When asked if she felt any limitations placed on her as a girl, Helen replied: "Never." She once asked her father if he would have preferred that she were a boy. "He said, 'That's silly! Girls are just as good as boys.' And he said, 'Besides, if you had been a boy, do you think I could have counted on that boy to do what you're doing for the family? You're just as good and just as smart.' He thought girls should be given the same opportunities, have the same kind of education as boys."

Right after high school, Helen got several housework jobs which, she said, "I didn't like at all." Then she got a job with the National Youth Administration, one of the many federal programs launched by President Franklin Roosevelt to put people to work in the 1930's. Helen worked at the Milwaukee Courthouse copying statistics from mortgage records and re-filing birth certificates. She found the work somewhat "useless," but earned $15-$20 per month. Part of the job required that she attend classes at vocational school, which she did, learning how to run a mimeograph machine among other skills.

In late 1939, at her father's suggestion, Helen signed up with the office workers' union. She had to take typing and shorthand tests to prove her abilities, and these Helen passed with flying colors. She was soon referred to a temporary job at the office of the Smith Steelworkers Local 19806, whose members built auto frames and rail ties for the A.O. Smith Corporation. She worked with another woman collecting dues, typing contracts and correspondence and doing light bookkeeping. Her starting pay was 60 cents per hour. The temporary job became a permanent one, and Helen worked for the Smith Steelworkers for the next 36 years.

A.O. Smith employed 3,000-4,000 people prior to the war, but after defense contracts poured in, the company hired thousands of new workers, bringing the ranks of Local 19806 to about 10,000. Among the new hires were some of the first women and African Americans ever employed at the plant. "We collected all the dues money over the counter," Helen said, "so I got to know a lot of people there, people who are still my friends today." Among them was Nellie Wilson, a lifelong friend who became an activist in the Steelworkers' union partly due to Helen's urging that she run for office. *(See chapter on Nellie Wilson)*

Helen was "lucky" in having two "wonderful bosses" during her years with the Steelworkers. The first, Felix Reisdorf, "was a man who was ahead of his times because he had no inhibitions about promoting women and giving us extra responsibilities. We were free to voice our opinions. He was just a great person to work for. I learned a great deal from him." The second, Bob Durkin, also built her confidence and broadened her responsibilities, including planning seminars for workers at the plants. "I was really surprised at the things I could do," Helen commented. "But if he hadn't had that confidence in me, I don't think I would have ventured even to offer to do that job."

Helen's earliest participation in her own local came when she joined the office workers' bowling team during the war years. Shortly thereafter she became a steward and in 1952 she was elected recording secretary of OPEIU Local 9, a position she held until 1975. She recalled that "until the 1970's we never had a grievance. We were extremely fortunate in having good people to work for." She sat on the Executive Board, which made policy for the local, and served on the joint negotiating committee for all the workers employed in union offices. Over the years, the committee helped to win improved contract language, wages and fringe benefits. "I think we did pretty well," she said. "I'm proud of the years I served on that negotiating committee."

Labor education played a role in fueling Helen's activism. In 1951, she won a scholarship from the State AFL to attend a labor institute for women at Sarah Lawrence College in New York. "I was so impressed about how they were trying to encourage and give women the confidence to run for office," she recalled. Later, Helen attended numerous classes at the University of Wisconsin-Extension School for Workers, both in Madison and Milwaukee. She praised Virginia Hart and other teachers for their "can do" attitude: "They made such an impression. They just made you feel that not only were you able to do it, you had a responsibility to go out there and do something for your sisters in the labor movement. It was very inspiring."

Helen Hensler ended up doing a great deal for her sisters in the labor movement. Among her most outstanding contributions was the establishment in 1970 of the Wisconsin State AFL-CIO Women's Committee — the first in the country — and its biennial women's conferences, which continue to be held to this day.

"The forming of the State AFL-CIO Women's Committee happened at a civil rights conference. I got there for lunch and had a couple of drinks. I remember sitting in the meeting in the afternoon when John Schmitt, who was president at the time, was bragging about the number of conferences the State AFL-CIO sponsors: educational, legislative, building trades and apprenticeship. And I remember Dolly Obrenovich sitting next to me and poking her and I said: 'Dolly, get up and ask why he doesn't sponsor a women's conference.' Dolly looked at me and said, 'I couldn't do that!' So I thought to myself, you stupid so-and-so, why don't you just get up and ask? So I did. It was good I'd had the two drinks, too, because that helped tremendously," Helen chuckled.

Helen Hensler

"I got up and I said, 'John, why hasn't the State AFL-CIO ever sponsored a women's conference?' And he said: 'Well, you gals, one thing, you never asked for it.' And I thought, well, that sounds logical to me. I don't recall anybody ever asking for it. And he says, 'Well, we'll have the secretary mark it down.' And I said to Dolly on the way out: 'Nothing is going to come from this.' This was in November 1969."

"Right before Christmas, John called me and said, 'Well, I'll tell you what Hensler, we're going to have a women's conference in March up in Wisconsin Rapids, and you and Lenore Hahlbeck can co-chair it.' Well here it was, Christmas, and we're having this conference in March in Wisconsin Rapids, and if you know anything about Wisconsin Rapids in winter — I thought, *'Oh my God!'* I had helped run some conferences for the union where I worked, but it's entirely different when you are just helping than when you are running it yourself. So Lenore and I got together and we decided that

"We took the position that anything that had to do with women was of concern to union women, and it still is."

we had to get workshops together and speakers. As I recall, we had all safe things like [workshops on] consumer protection and parliamentary procedure but not really anything on just specific women's issues. I guess we felt we didn't want to rock the boat too much."

The committee grew bolder, however. "We took the position that anything that had to do with women was of concern to union women, and it still is," Helen said. "We were the first State AFL-CIO Women's Committee that went on record in support of the Equal Rights Amendment, which I'm very proud of because we did this when the AFL-CIO was still opposed to it." Helen explained: "When any committee passes a resolution it goes to the Executive Board of the State AFL-CIO and finally to the convention itself for approval.... So the State AFL-CIO goes on record in support of the ERA and it comes up at the convention and it passes. The Women's Committee was just

Like Our Sisters Before Us

Pioneering Sisters: Members of the Wisconsin State AFL-CIO Women's Committee at the first women's conference in Wisconsin Rapids on March 7, 1970. Front row, l-r: Marcella Dougherty, State, County and Municipal Employees (SCME) # 1280, Oshkosh; Helen Hensler, Office and Professional Employees International Union # 9, Milwaukee; Lenore Hahlbeck, Bakery and Confectionery Workers # 205, Milwaukee; Anita Thom, Printing Pressmen, # 662, Eau Claire. Middle row, l-r: Rose Marie Baron, SCME # 1954, Milwaukee; Rosella Wartner, Marathon County Labor Council, Wausau; Irene Henderson, Communications Workers of America, # 5500, Milwaukee; Connie Miller, Meat Cutters # 538, Madison; Bernice Reck, Kenosha County Labor Council, Kenosha. Upper row, l-r: Sharon Kobza, Service Employees International # 292, Wisconsin Rapids; Nellie Wilson, State AFL-CIO Representative, Milwaukee; Ann Stockman, Allied Industrial Workers (AIW) # 232, Milwaukee; Florence Simons, AIW # 322, Milwaukee. June Michelfelder of SCME # 1 in Milwaukee, another original committee member, is not pictured.

beyond themselves to think that we pulled that off!" Such pressure from the grass-roots led the national AFL-CIO to reverse its position on the ERA in 1973.

"We had good turnouts at every single women's conference," Helen said. "At some we had over 300 [participants]. Women really needed this kind of an outlet." Because many women could not get elected to attend other conferences, the women's conferences were often the first in which they participated. Helen said that women who had gone to other conferences felt "they were run by men, they were dominated by men, and sometimes if they got up to ask a question they were made to feel foolish. That did not happen at women's conferences. They felt it was easier to speak and participate."

"I think the years I served as chair of the Women's Committee were some of the most rewarding and fulfilling of my union career," Helen declared. (She had assumed the position of chair upon the death of Lenore Hahlbeck and maintained it until 1986.) "I just felt I touched so many women in one way or another, and then when I see that some of these same women later ran for office — they got to know that there were other women doing these things and they could do them too."

"Men are not going to do it for us," Helen advised. "We have to learn how to play the game. Women have to learn that we have to get in there, we have to fight, we have to organize amongst ourselves and work so we get each other elected to office. Now it has greatly improved. There are a lot more women on negotiating committees. There are more women on International staffs. There are women serving as business agents. So there have been great strides."

"I was also involved in the founding conference of the Coalition of Labor Union Women in Chicago in 1974. That was a big conference [over 3,000 women] — auto workers, farm workers, office workers, women in trades — and they were all gung-ho as to what they thought should be done. It really is a wonderful concept because it brings together women from all unions throughout the country. They didn't even have to be affiliated with the AFL-CIO. All these women had the chance to meet and voice their concerns, set up some policies and goals. As a result of that, chapters were set up and I was involved in the Milwaukee chapter right from the start."

During this same period of feminist activism in the 1970's, Helen was appointed by Gov. Patrick J. Lucey to the Wisconsin Governor's

Commission on the Status of Women. The Commission advocated reforms on a variety of issues that impacted women, including pay equity, affirmative action, marital property reform and domestic violence. "That was a rewarding experience for me," Helen said, "because I was not only involved with union women. I was involved with women from all spectrums of life from all over the state. There were farm women and welfare women and professional women. It certainly enriched my life a great deal by having this opportunity. It also convinced me that union women had a lot to offer on the Commission itself."

"To tell you the truth," Helen confided conspiratorially, "we union women are much better organized than almost any other group of women. We are geared that way. We're taught that way and we believe in structure. We like to have things organized well." Kathryn Clarenbach, chair of the state commission, recognized these skills in Helen and convinced her to run for treasurer of the National Association of Commissions for Women.

> *"We union women are much better organized than almost any other group of women. We are geared that way."*

She served on its board and as its treasurer from 1972 to 1978. On both the state commission and the national association, Helen said, "It gave me a lot of satisfaction to give the union and working women's standpoint. Some of them," she said, referring to the professional women members, "had a lot to learn about us."

In her own work life, Helen left her job at the Smith Steelworkers' union in 1976 to take the job of office manager at Iron Workers Local 471. She retired from that job in 1993 only to take up the challenge of being business representative for the still struggling Local 9. She expressed pride at being able to assist the union that had given her so much. She retired permanently in 1997.

Looking back on her union career, Helen singled out for praise her labor colleague Catherine Conroy and educator Kathryn Clarenbach, both of whom provided her with valuable support and

Helen Hensler

opportunities for growth. She also credited her sister, Evelyn Hoover, who worked with Helen at Smith Steelworkers and later as office secretary at Local 9. "You have to have somebody you trust implicitly," Helen said. "Evelyn was the one person I could always count on as being there for me — be it good or bad times. She was the best friend I ever had." Evelyn passed away in 1997.

"I don't have too many regrets in my life," Helen said. "I feel I've been very fortunate. I've lived a very fulfilling life. Through the labor movement I've met some of my best friends. I enjoyed every bit, the good and the bad times. There were [more] better times than bad, and the bad times were a learning experience. I'm just happy I could make some small contribution along the way."

Helen Hensler, 1989

JOANNE BRUCH

*"I attended union meetings more religiously
than I attended church.
To me, it was church work."*

Nothing in her youth really predicted the important role Whitewater's Joanne Bruch eventually played in her union. That her union career began with her hiring as a strikebreaker — albeit an unwitting one — makes her story even more amazing. Joanne herself has attributed her decades of activism to "serendipity," which Webster's dictionary defines as "the gift of finding valuable or agreeable things not sought for."

The record shows that in the 16 years she spent as an assembler at Whitewater Electronics (1964-80), Joanne held nearly every position in Local 1032 of the International Union of Electronic, Electrical, Salaried, Machine and Furniture Workers (IUE) — steward, recording secretary, trustee, vice-president and president. She served on the Executive Board of IUE District 8 (1972-80) and was a field secretary for the International (1980-89) as well as an International representative for Wisconsin from 1989 until her retirement in 1991. Were all these achievements just the result of "serendipity?"

Joanne Bruch

Joanne was born in Waukesha on August 12, 1935 and had the distinction of being the biggest baby born at Waukesha Memorial Hospital to that date, weighing in at 11½ pounds. Her father, James Larson, was a foundry worker at the time, though he later went back to his roots as a farmer. Her mother, Eleanor Perry Larson, was a descendant of Commodore Oliver Hazard Perry, who defeated the British in the Battle of Lake Erie in 1813. When her three children reached high school age, Eleanor took classes of her own and found work as a secretary in Fort Atkinson.

Joanne graduated from Whitewater High School in 1953. The long bus ride back and forth and chores at home on the farm prevented her from participating in extra-curricular activities, which was a disappointment. But Joanne thoroughly enjoyed the farm life, and she and the other farm kids "hung out together." After chores, she said, "everyone met and swam at Turtle Lake. We had all kinds of good times."

> *"I'd wanted to have twelve kids, but by the time I'd had six I realized how expensive it was and all the work it entailed!"*

After graduation, Joanne got a job at the Fort Atkinson Hospital as a nurse's aide. She was awarded a scholarship for three years of nursing school on the condition that she return to the hospital to practice nursing, but she declined the offer. "At that time I was dating and thinking of getting married and setting up a home and having a family," Joanne explained. "So I kind of muffed up on that one. But in the long run, everything turned out alright anyway."

Joanne met her husband, Harry Bruch, while caring for his brother in the hospital. Harry was about to be discharged from the military after serving in Korea. Like Joanne, he was from a farm family, and he looked forward to settling down and starting his own. The couple was married in October, 1954 and, by 1963, produced six children: Arlene, Kathleen, Steven, Paulene, Jennifer and Janis. "I'd wanted to have twelve kids, but by the time I'd had six I realized how expensive it was and all the work it entailed!" Joanne said.

Like Our Sisters Before Us

Joanne and Harry faced many difficult challenges in the first ten years of their marriage. Within months of the ceremony, both were laid off from their jobs. The house and car they purchased with Harry's muster money and proceeds from the sale of some horses were repossessed. They moved to Kenosha where Harry found work at American Motors, but after a few months he was laid off again. They then moved in with Joanne's parents while they searched for work. "Jobs were like hen's teeth," Joanne said. "They just weren't around."

In 1956, the Bruchs went to work for relatives on a farm near Hebron. They stayed several years and bought an interest in some Holstein cows which they hoped would be the nucleus of their own dairy herd. In 1960, they moved to another farm where Harry made a 50-50 deal to live-in and work the farm for its owner. But problems with flooded land and differences with the owner over how to manage the farm and livestock resulted in financial losses. The Bruchs were forced to declare bankruptcy in 1963. At about that time, Harry came down with bleeding ulcers, and Joanne was pregnant for the sixth time. Joanne "begged, borrowed and stole from anyone that I could" to support the kids while Harry recovered. "It was just a terrible, terrible time," she said.

Joanne heard through the bankruptcy attorney of a job at Whitewater Electronics, where she worked that summer. Harry, meanwhile, was hired at a factory in Libertyville, Illinois. But it was only a brief respite from their trials. Harry wasn't happy working in Illinois and decided to try farming again. Joanne recalled the next year of tenant farming as "a steady downhill slide" during which the family worked hard but made little money and was forced to live in "rat traps" with bad plumbing. The last straw for Joanne was having to share a house with other tenants. "*Anything* would have been better than what we had," she said in retrospect.

One day, Joanne took the grocery money Harry gave her and used most of it to rent a house in Whitewater. When she returned home and told Harry what she'd done, he was appalled. "You *what!?*" he yelled. It was a radical step for someone raised to be an obedient wife, but Joanne stood her ground. "I'm going and I'm gonna live there, and you can come along if you want or you can stay here, but I am not going to farm anymore!" she told him.

Joanne Bruch

Joanne Bruch and her husband, Harry, about 1970

Joanne's gamble paid off. Harry got another farming job and worked out a deal for the owner to pay the rent on the Bruchs' house in the city. Joanne was re-hired at Whitewater Electronics, and a year later Harry got a job at Hawthorne-Melody, the dairy company. Within a few years of moving to Whitewater and obtaining steady employment, the Bruch family was on much sounder financial footing.

The assembly job at Whitewater Electronics was a "revelation" to Joanne: "God, that was such a great feeling to know that I was now a productive human being! Whatever money I'd gotten in the ten years I was married up to this point was money that he [Harry] doled out to me that had a special place to go. When I earned that first paycheck and I came home, though I knew that check was gonna be for groceries, it also provided me with the ability to say, 'I earned it, and though I'm gonna spend it for groceries, I can spend it the way I want.'"

Joanne said that during the year she worked in the hospital, her parents told her how she should spend her earnings. "Then I got married and had these children, and I was told how to act, how to talk, how to dress — everything. But when I went to work [at Whitewater Electronics] and I saw how those other people were, it was just like a flower blooming in the spring. All of a sudden I could talk to somebody and not be put down. I found out I had a brain and, given the opportunity, it could think. It was a real change for us. It changed our whole lives together. It was a real adjustment and it continued to be a real adjustment for him for a long time."

> **"When I went to work....it was like a flower blooming in the spring."**

"About two or three days after I started there," Joanne said, "the supervisor came up to me and said, 'If there's no contract by March 1st, don't be afraid to come to work because my husband is a City of Whitewater policeman and he'll be happy to escort you across the picket line.' Well, let me tell you, when she said that, I really got nervous. Because I didn't know what a union was, I didn't know what a picket line was, I didn't understand a contract. I didn't understand any of those terms. To me — this was a job."

Co-workers referred Joanne and a few other new hires to the president and chief steward of Local 1032. "They explained to us what was coming off," Joanne said. "They were in contract negotiations and we were probably hired as scabs. Then they explained to us what scabs were. It was my very first time I had ever heard that. So every break for about a week or two, they came to us or we went to them and we'd get some more education about what was going on."

Harry warned Joanne not to get involved, but she joined the union anyway and began attending meetings. Eventually, "I attended union meetings more religiously than I attended church," she said. "To me, it *was* church work." The immediate crisis was defused when the contract was ratified, but the episode was a dramatic introduction to unionism for Joanne.

Initially, Joanne worked on the line assembling coils for televisions, but her first year of employment at Whitewater Electronics was characterized by repeated lay-offs and call-backs. She transferred to the mechanical filter department at the company's plant in Fort Atkinson, where the pace was less hectic and, a supervisor told her, she was less likely to be laid off. Within a few months of working there, Local 1032's chief steward asked Joanne if she'd like to be a steward for the 25 workers in Fort Atkinson. "She tried to minimize the job by saying that I was just going to be the eyes and ears for the union," Joanne recalled, "so I ran and got elected."

Joanne admitted feeling "fumbuzzled" when filing her first grievance on behalf of a worker. She wasn't sure what to do or say, and in her first meeting with the company she was "all thumbs and red-faced." Joanne credited Local 1032 President Ruth Burhans and the chief steward for teaching her the ropes and building her confidence.

"I developed good friends and relationships at work," she commented. "Early on, I realized I found my niche. Not the factory job — though I loved the work and the people — but working and helping others through my union affiliation really satisfied me, whet my appetite for knowledge and, I hope, made me a better person."

Joanne had indeed found her niche, because after being steward for awhile, she was elected recording secretary of her local. She also became a delegate to IUE District 8, which includes Wisconsin, Michigan, Illinois and Indiana, and later a member of District 8's Executive Board. Through her participation on the Executive Board, she learned about the work of the IUE on a broader scale. When the sitting president of Local 1032 passed away unexpectedly in 1973, Joanne was "serendipitously" elected president of her local.

Local 1032, whose membership topped off at about 300, had a pretty good relationship with the company, according to Joanne. She recalled only one case where a grievance was taken all the way to arbitration. In negotiations, she said, "We could always manage to talk them into seeing things our way contractually, though they never could give us the money we thought we deserved." Joanne herself started at $1.10 an hour. When the company folded 16 years later, she was making $3.50. "We had a good vacation schedule, we had bonus days for those people who had seniority. We had good benefits, but we didn't make money worth a damn."

Joanne acknowledged that the majority of workers at Whitewater Electronics were women, but she couldn't say for sure the low pay scale was due to sex discrimination. Male workers were paid at the same equally low rates. "It was just an issue of poor management," Joanne said. "[The owner] had gone into bankruptcy before I had worked there. He overloaded the management side and paid them very well, and there wasn't a whole lot of money left over for the production people.... One time we negotiated and we got three cents on the hour and we thought we had done just fantastic. Can you imagine, *three cents on the hour?*"

The "poor management" Joanne cited apparently contributed to the sale and subsequent closing of the plant in 1980: "They watched the television industry go overseas and go down the tubes and they never bothered to diversify. When they finally decided to do something about getting other types of work in, they were a day late and a dollar short." As president of Local 1032, Joanne was deeply involved in negotiating the closing settlement which members had little choice but to accept.

During those final negotiations, the IUE representatives assisting Local 1032 announced an opening for a field secretary at the Wisconsin IUE office. Knowledge of and commitment to unions was a requirement. In another of the many examples of "serendipity" in her life, Joanne applied for and accepted the job. Harry, worried the job would require travel, paid a call on IUE representative Larry Kitzinger to see what the job entailed. But Joanne was determined to have the job, whether Harry approved or not.

"Financially, we were committed to two incomes, and so I knew I had to continue to work," Joanne said. The job not only tripled her previous income, but offered a pension plan, a "big incentive" for Joanne who was at that time 45 years old. In addition, she noted, "I wanted to stay in the union movement. I never had belonged to any union other than the IUE so my loyalty was to the IUE. I wanted to continue developing my mind, learning, doing all those things that had become second nature to me."

Joanne had just one month between the time Whitewater Electronics closed and her new job began. During that time, she said, "I had a wedding for one of my daughters, I got a driver's license, I bought a car and rented a typewriter." Worried that her high school typing skills needed refreshing, Joanne practiced typing late at night after the rest of the family was asleep.

Joanne Bruch

With the help of Kitzinger and Tom Rebman, the two International representatives, Joanne survived her initial butterflies and mastered the office machines and much more. Eventually, she said, "I went in on contract negotiations with them. I worked organizing campaigns with them. I helped with arbitrations. I did every aspect of what a staff rep would do. And I learned so much. Every day was a learning experience when I came to work with those guys. They were just really, really helpful to me."

In 1989, when Kitzinger retired and Rebman became secretary-treasurer of District 8, they recommended that Joanne be named the IUE staff representative for Wisconsin. She held that position until her retirement two and a half years later. At that time, IUE had ten locals in the state with between 2,500 and 3,000 members. Joanne assisted the locals with all aspects of their operations: negotiating contracts, handling grievances, filing charges with the National Labor Relations Board, helping with financial records, officer elections, arbitration hearings — "whatever they needed." She logged between 30,000 and 50,000 miles yearly in her work.

Joanne Bruch, 1991

Like Our Sisters Before Us

A smaller but interesting part of the job involved lobbying legislators about relevant legislation, like a bill to ban replacement workers during strikes, the Family and Medical Leave Act, and national health care. "Organized labor is small compared to the number of people actually working," Joanne said. "When we go there [the State Capitol or the US Congress] and lobby those people, I feel we're lobbying for *all* workers, not just organized labor."

She noted the hard knocks labor has taken since the 1980's: "I felt very strongly at the time that Reagan de-certified PATCO [the Professional Air Traffic Controllers Organization], we should have shut this country down. That gave a signal to companies that the companies could do almost anything they wanted to the labor force and it would be sanctioned by government. We should never have allowed that message to go unchallenged."

When asked whether she experienced sexism as a woman union leader, Joanne said she "never" felt it at the local level because so many officers of Local 1032 had been women who provided good role models and encouragement. She did experience some sexist attitudes when she was the only woman on the Executive Board of District 8, as well as from officers of a few locals who doubted her leadership as their representative. "[Did] I let that bother me?" she asked. "No." By maintaining her professionalism, she felt sure they'd "come around." In her work at District 8, Joanne met many "very qualified" women serving as presidents of locals whom she encouraged to run for the Executive Board.

Joanne retired on July 1, 1991. Only days later she learned she had breast cancer. She had surgery and chemotherapy and had a "rough time" for about three years. By early 1998, she had been free of cancer for five years. "Of course, you can tell people," she said. "We always hear about the statistics and the people who die. It's important for everyone to hear about how many of us survive."

She and Harry are both retired. They've spent many months on the road in their 30' trailer seeing the country. Joanne describes herself as a "retiree activist." She chairs the retirees' group for IUE District 8, is recording secretary for the Wisconsin Council of Senior Citizens and is active in the Democratic Party. She even finds time to help out as a cook in her son-in-law's restaurant in Sullivan. "I've kept myself very involved and busy. What else would I do?" she asked.

FLORENCE SIMONS

"If I felt that I was right,
I didn't kow-tow to the company, you know?
I felt they had to listen."

Florence Helfrich Simons, the daughter of a "strong union man," was a union activist most of her life. At the Milwaukee Lace Paper Co. (1934-42), she participated in the organizing drive and sit-down strike that secured recognition of the International Association of Machinists' (IAM) local at the plant. At Globe Union and then Centralab (1942-84), she was the recording secretary for the United Auto Workers/Allied Industrial Workers (AIW) Local 322 from 1948-80, and president of AIW Local 765 from 1982-84. For 26 years, Simons was secretary-treasurer of AIW District Council 9. She was a founding member of the Coalition of Labor Union Women and played a significant role on the State AFL-CIO Women's Committee.

Florence was born May 1, 1914 in Milwaukee to Anton Helfrich and Anna Maria Habach Helfrich, immigrants who came to the U.S. from Germany at the turn of the century. The youngest of five children, Florence joked: "I was the postscript." Her father worked in the breweries until his marriage, operated a saloon for several years and then became an independent contractor doing masonry, carpentry and remodeling work. Mother held down the home front, raising the children and tending to boarders.

Anton Helfrich was "a strong believer in unions" who had been a member of the brewery workers' local and who, as a contractor, hired only union workers. "He just didn't want anybody but a union man on his job," Florence noted. "I really had that sort of ingrained in me right from an early age, that one should not only belong to a union if one worked in a place that was organized, but that one should always support unions too, as he did, by hiring union help."

Florence recalled a happy youth at least until the time of the Great Depression: "We had a difficult time because those were not easy years to make a living," she said. "But, at the same time, I don't think of us as living in poverty. No matter how little my father made, my mother always seemed to know how to manage the kitchen and keep everyone well-fed."

Florence graduated from North Division High School in 1931. "When I graduated, it was just a month after my 17th birthday, so I was very young and places just wouldn't hire me. I ended up taking care of children, doing housework for people." In one such housework job, she rose at 5:00 in the morning to prepare the family breakfast and often did not get a chance to rest until 7:30 or 8:00 in the evening. "I wasn't supposed to be idle

> *"Housework was a terrible line of work to be doing if you have any idea of what is right and wrong, just or unjust."*

at all," she noted. Housework was, she said, "a terrible line of work to be doing if you have any idea of what is right and wrong, just or unjust. I felt exploited whenever I did that."

She managed to find part-time work at Kresge's dime store and at Schuster's department store during Christmas time and, in 1934, was hired at the Schlitz Brewery during the first rush of production after Prohibition ended. Florence, a member of the brewery workers' union, worked as an inspector in the bottle house and later as a packer in the warehouse. After several months she was laid off, but she got a tip about full-time job openings at Milwaukee Lace Paper Co. and was hired there. Her non-unionized job involved trimming doilies and other paper products.

"In 1934 or 1935, the toolroom there organized with the International Association of Machinists," Florence explained. "I don't know how many toolmakers there were [at Milwaukee Lace Paper], let's say a dozen. They couldn't get very far if they were the only ones organized there because if they had labor trouble and all of us were not organized at all, we had no contract clause that would prevent us from going through their picket line if they had a strike.... So the toolroom organized [the production workers] and we joined the IAM. I belonged until I left there in 1942."

But the establishment of the IAM at Milwaukee Lace Paper was not without difficulties. In 1937, contract negotiations broke down over wages and seniority issues. This occurred at the height of the big "sit-down" strikes in the auto industry, when workers refused to work but remained in the plant. Florence and fellow workers voted for their own sit-down strike against Milwaukee Lace Paper, a strike which lasted for a week. At the time, Florence worked at the company's Commerce Street warehouse with three female and eight male co-workers. It was agreed that the men would occupy the warehouse overnight while the women would sneak in by day, bringing supplies for the men. Florence recalled whiling away the worktime hours playing cards, reading newspapers and feeling excited about being part of a national labor movement. The workers won their demands, and Florence did not recall that the company took any disciplinary action against them.

When World War II intensified, the demand for delicate paper products declined, and the workers at Milwaukee Lace Paper were reduced to two or three day work weeks. Florence picked up extra income as a clerk at Sendik's produce market while she looked for a new job. In November 1942, she began work at Globe Union, which was swamped with work from defense contracts. Globe Union specialized in battery production. Florence worked for several years in the silver mica assembly department and then, for more than three decades, as a timekeeper. At that time, Globe Union workers were affiliated with the AFL's United Auto Workers' union (which later evolved into the Allied Industrial Workers), and Florence immediately inquired about joining: "I wouldn't think of working in a plant where there was a union and not joining it," she declared.

The demands of war production kept workers very busy, but a labor dispute developed toward the end of the war. Negotiations broke down and, in September 1945, Globe Union workers went out on a strike that lasted five months. Calling it a "long, tough haul," Florence remembered weeks of picketing at the Keefe Avenue plant and the company's corporate headquarters in downtown Milwaukee. Resolving the conflict was complicated, she said, by the involvement of the War Labor Board, whose job it was to oversee labor relations during the war years. Members of Florence's local voted to continue the picketing and bargaining while at the same time accepting temporary jobs. For several months during the strike, Florence worked at the Great Lakes Naval Station processing military discharges.

When the strike ended and Florence returned to work, she was assigned to timekeeping duties. "What we did was to actually go around to everybody's workplace to record what they were doing, what rates they were on, whether it was daywork or piecework, and they filled in count information. When I got the cards the next morning, I had to compute their point earnings — what percent of the hourly rate they were earning on whatever rates they were working on. Even that was not enough to keep me busy all day so my boss, the paymaster, asked if I'd mind helping out in payroll. I figured vacation pay. I totaled earnings. I did a lot of things."

Did her work as a timekeeper create any conflicts with fellow workers? "No, I don't think it caused any real problems. I just felt that if I did my job truthfully and honestly it couldn't be faulted."

In 1948, Florence ran for and was elected recording secretary of her local, a position she held until 1982. As recording secretary, she automatically had a seat on the bargaining committee, where she became immersed in grievances and biennial contract negotiations. The union sent her to the School for Workers in Madison to take courses in time study and job evaluation. "For a long time, I was the only one with any substantial training in time study and job evaluation, so whenever we had a grievance in either of those areas, I had to be called in to go over the company's studies.... We had a lot of troubles on rates because we had mostly piecework operations. It required a lot of looking into."

Another problematic area at Globe Union was job segregation and unequal pay based on sex. Although the majority of workers were women, men dominated certain departments — punch press, screw machine and battery — and were paid more than women even when they held the same jobs.

"There had been many problems, contractually, in the workplace about being a man or a woman," Florence conceded. "For instance, for many years there were two wage schedules. A man, even in the lowest grade, would not start at the lowest grade a woman could. He was three or four steps higher.

> *"For many years we had two wage schedules. A man, even in the lowest grade, would not start at the lowest grade a woman could."*

If a woman was paid Class 23 for a job, if a man were put on that he would be paid Class 26. That was immediate discrimination, and it was quite a few years before we got rid of that.... Union pressure and, of course, Title VII [of the Civil Rights Act of 1964 which prohibited employment discrimination based on sex] came in there [to end the practice]."

Florence served as co-editor of the union newsletter, *The Round Globe*, in the late 1940's. The most popular feature was the "Orchids and Onions" column in which the editors either commended or condemned company practices. "One time we really raked them over the coals about that parking lot, and it wasn't more than two weeks when they re-paved the whole thing," Florence noted with satisfaction. Another time, someone from the company requested copies of *The Round Globe* for board members. "Apparently, the Board of Directors wanted to see what was wrong with the place and wanted to see the latest "Orchids and Onions," Florence said wryly.

Florence described her attitude toward the company: "If I felt that I was right, I didn't kow-tow to the company, you know? I felt they had to listen. It was their obligation and I made them listen. You don't win every case like that, but at least they have some respect for you then, and I think the company did."

Like Our Sisters Before Us

At one time, a supervisor tried to buy off Florence by offering to make timekeeping a salaried, but non-union, position. She suspected he was trying to silence her because of her recent testimony about the company's unfair labor practices, so she rebuffed him in a way that emphasized her loyalty to the union. "I don't intend to get involved bargaining over this issue when I've got a committee to do it for me," she told him. But the company did succeed in buying off some workers. "When people have families, no matter where their hearts are, they often choose to vote their pocketbook," Florence commented.

Florence Simons, 1990

Florence Simons

In her decades of union service, Florence witnessed people she called company "toadies" who attempted to buy off, spy on and/or intimidate union leaders. She saw contracts gradually balloon from one or two page documents to 70-80 page booklets whose increasingly technical language necessitated the hiring of attorneys. She was encouraged by the growing numbers of women who became active in their unions. She recalled attending her International's convention in 1951 and being one of only six female delegates among the 500 in attendance. By the 1980's, she said, there were "many, many more women participating."

She felt one of her most important contributions was as a member of the Wisconsin Advisory Committee on Women and Child Labor in the 1960's. There, Florence argued vehemently against a lower minimum wage for minors and restaurant workers. "We didn't just talk about wages, we talked quite a bit about safety.... At times, legislators would appear before the committee, especially if they had problems with parts of the law. They then asked us to look at it and advise changes. We sometimes had people there from the university who had done research in different areas that might affect the question. So it was interesting in that respect."

On the Advisory Committee, Florence said, "It became apparent to me why so many employers could legally discriminate against women — because it was written right into the law. So many things, like not allowing a woman to work alone on a shift. Our plant wouldn't put any women on the third shift, and sometimes that's the only time a woman *can* work. So a lot of those laws, although they were allegedly protective, they were also discriminatory. The law actually gave employers additional excuses for paying women less, and I think they exploited them as much as they could. After Title VII, some of the [discriminatory] parts of state law were automatically outlawed because they were contrary to federal legislation. So that changed a lot."

In 1970, Florence became a founder and charter member of the Wisconsin State AFL-CIO Women's Committee. She helped organize its biennial conferences, often participating in panels and workshops. She also attended the founding convention of the Coalition of Labor Union Women in Chicago in 1974 and was an officer in the Milwaukee chapter of CLUW for many years.

Like Our Sisters Before Us

Florence urged women to increase their influence in unions by getting involved in committee work and running for office. Instead of relying on the "old boys' network," unions should practice open hiring of business agents and organizers so women become aware of those opportunities. In addition, "I think there should be more encouragement for women to run as delegates to conventions, because the more women who go each time, the closer we will come to the day when more women are going to be elected to top offices in the Internationals, because those elections are held at those conventions among the delegates who attend. If locals always send men, who's going to be elected? It's going to have to start right down at the local level. It's not a matter of trickle down; it's a matter of feeding up."

Florence expressed only two regrets. "I wish we could have gotten a union shop a lot sooner. The company didn't even agree to check-off of dues until the late 1950's. They were deathly opposed to anything smacking of a union shop." The union shop was not secured until 1982, only after Centralab, the company's electronics division, was sold to North American Phillips. (This also resulted in the splitting of AIW Local 322's membership into separate locals, 322 and 765. Florence served as Local 765's president from 1982 until her retirement two years later.)

"I think when you give so much time something has to suffer," she added. "I think my home life suffered a little bit. My husband [William] was more patient than I had a right to expect. But we were always able to talk out our differences."

Florence didn't hesitate when asked about the most satisfying part of her union work. "The people I have met and grown to know," she said. "The exchange of ideas is what I think is rewarding. Nowhere else would I have met someone like Catherine Conroy or Helen Hensler or Nellie Wilson — that's reward in itself."

After her retirement in 1984, Florence remained active in AIW's retirees' group, in its committee on human rights and in the Wisconsin AFL-CIO Women's Committee. In the months prior to her death on March 11, 1994, she followed closely the merger of her beloved Allied Industrial Workers with the United Paperworkers International Union. She had studied the issue thoroughly and was content in knowing the merger would create a stronger union.

List of Interviewees

The following is a complete list of all the women interviewed for the *Women of Wisconsin Labor Oral History Project*. The list includes their primary union affiliation(s), their hometowns and the dates on which they were interviewed. All of the audio recordings and supporting materials are housed in the Archives Division of the State Historical Society of Wisconsin.

Helen Altstadt - Office and Professional Employees International Union, Milwaukee: September 29, 1989

Mary Ann Braithwaite - Wisconsin Federation of Teachers/ American Federation of Teachers, La Crosse: August 31 and September 24, 1993

Joanne Bruch - International Union of Electronic, Electrical, Salaried, Machine and Furniture Workers, Whitewater: April 15, 1991

Catherine Conroy - Communications Workers of America, Milwaukee: May 18 and 25, June 30 and July 13, 1988

Ann Crump - Communications Workers of America, Milwaukee: March 3 and 15, April 20, and September 27, 1993

Like Our Sisters Before Us

Evelyn Donner Day - International Ladies' Garment Workers Union and United Auto Workers, Milwaukee: February 1, 1990

Evelyn Gotzion - Federal Labor Union 19587 and United Auto Workers, Madison: August 18, 1992

Verona Guinn - Firemen and Oilers, Milwaukee: June 1, 1992, January 17, 1994

Helen Hensler - Office and Professional Employees International Union, Milwaukee: November 11 and 24, 1988 and June 13, 1989

Nancy Hoffmann - Plumbers, Milwaukee: April 22, 1992 and September 27, 1993

Alice Holz - Office and Professional Employees International Union, Milwaukee: June 27 and July 6 and 20, 1989

Evelyn Hunholz - Women's Auxiliary, Milwaukee: March 6, 1990

Dorothy Jafferis - Office and Professional Employees International Union, Madison: October 25, 1990

Judith Kuhn - A founder of Milwaukee Women in the Trades, Milwaukee: September 1 and 15, 1992

Martha Love - American Federation of State, County and Municipal Employees, Milwaukee: February 17 and 23, and August 20, 1993

Candice Owley - Wisconsin Federation of Nurses and Health Professionals/American Federation of Teachers, Milwaukee: May 12 and June 18 and 29, 1993

Cecilia Peterson - Amalgamated Transit Union, Milwaukee: June 10 and July 1, 1992

Like Our Sisters Before Us

Darina Rasmussen - Amalgamated Clothing Workers of America and Office and Professional Employees International Union, Milwaukee: June 22, 1990

Lee Schmeling - Graphic Arts International Union and Graphic Communications International Union, Neenah: April 14, 1993

Florence Simons - International Association of Machinists, United Auto Workers, Allied Industrial Workers, Milwaukee: November 17 and December 12, 1989

Leona Tarnowski - United Packinghouse Workers of America and United Food and Commercial Workers, Milwaukee: July 15, 1992

Doris Thom - International Association of Machinists and United Auto Workers, Janesville: October 9, 1990

Rosella Wartner - Federal Labor Union 20690 and International Brotherhood of Electrical Workers, Wausau: March 4, 1995

Nellie Wilson - Smith Steelworkers, Milwaukee: August 3 and 17, and September 8, 1989

Patricia Yunk - American Federation of State, County and Municipal Employees, Milwaukee: November 3 and December 2, 1992

Joan Zeiger - American Federation of State, County and Municipal Employees, Milwaukee: March 3, 1991

Ronnie Gilbert, the singer/ actress best known for her work with the folk group The Weavers, was also interviewed for the project. She is not a Wisconsin native but was performing her one-woman musical play *"Mother Jones: The Most Dangerous Woman in America"* in Milwaukee in 1992. She is a member of the American Federation of Television and Radio Artists and Actors Equity.

Bibliography

HOW TO CONDUCT ORAL HISTORY INTERVIEWS

Brown, Cynthia Stokes. **Like It Was: A Complete Guide to Writing Oral History.** New York: Teachers and Writers Collaborative, 1988

Davis, Cullom and MacLean, Kay. **Oral History From Tape to Type.** Chicago: American Library Association, 1977

Kornbluh, Joyce L. and Mikusko, M. Brady. **Working Womenroots: An Oral History Primer.** Ann Arbor, Michigan: Institute of Labor and Industrial Relations, University of Michigan, 1980

Sitton, Thad and Mehaffy, George L., et al. **Oral History: A Guide for Teachers and Others.** Austin: University of Texas Press, 1983

MORE ON WOMEN'S LABOR HISTORY

Jones, Mary Harris. **The Autobiography of Mother Jones.** Chicago: Charles H. Kerr Publishing Co., 1974 (1925)

Kessler-Harris, Alice. **Out to Work: A History of Wage-Earning Women in the U.S.** New York: Oxford University Press, 1982

Kornbluh, Joyce L. and O'Farrell, Brigid, Eds. **Rocking the Boat: Union Women's Voices, 1915-1975.** New Brunswick, NJ: Rutgers University Press, 1996

Milkman, Ruth, Ed. **Women, Work and Protest: A Century of U.S. Women's Labor History.** Boston: Routledge & Kegan Paul, 1985

Wertheimer, Barbara Mayer. **We Were There: The Story of Working Women in America.** New York: Pantheon Books, 1977

Photo Credits

Evelyn Donner Day: All photos courtesy of Charles and Marilyn Donner

Alice Holz: p. 13, from the book **White Collar Union: The Story of the OPEIU and Its People** by Joseph E. Finley. Used with permission of the OPEIU; p. 15, by Murray Weiss

Evelyn Gotzion: p. 20, photo by Marny Malin

Catherine Conroy: p. 28, Wisconsin State AFL-CIO; pp. 31 and 33, *The Milwaukee Journal-Sentinel*, July 9, 1978 and October 16, 1974

Nellie Wilson: pp. 39 and 40, photos courtesy of Nellie Wilson; p. 45, by Murray Weiss

Doris Thom: p. 47, courtesy of Doris Thom; p. 52, by Murray Weiss

Lee Schmeling: p. 59, *Neenah-Menasha Daily Northwestern*, May 12, 1977; p. 60, by Marny Malin

Helen Hensler: pp. 64 and 68, courtesy of Helen Hensler; p. 71, by Murray Weiss

Joanne Bruch: p. 75, courtesy of Joanne Bruch; p. 79, by Murray Weiss

Florence Simons: p. 86, by Murray Weiss

About the Author

*Jamakaya is a writer and historian who has documented the feminist, labor and gay and lesbian communities in Milwaukee for 25 years. From 1979 to 1982, she was Publisher and Editor of **Amazon: Milwaukee's Feminist Press**. Her column "Sisternews and Views" appeared in the **Wisconsin Light** for many years. Her work has been published in papers throughout Wisconsin and the US. In 1995, she was the recipient of the Progressive Milwaukee Award for her ongoing coverage of the city's activist groups. Jamakaya lives on Milwaukee's east side with her partner and their two cats, Xena and Angel.*